# Research Writing Using Traditional and Electronic Sources

Nancy L. Joseph

Oakland University

Prentice Hall, Upper Saddle River, New Jersey 07458

*Library of Congress Cataloging-in-Publication Data*

JOSEPH, NANCY L. (date)
    Research writing using traditional and electronic sources / Nancy
L. Joseph
       p.   cm.

    Includes bibliographical references (p.  ) and index.
    ISBN  0–13–633058–4
    1. Report writing.  2. Research—Methodology.  3. Citation of
electronic information resources.  I. Title.
LB2369.J64  1999
808'.02—dc21                         98–41713
                                        CIP

Editorial Director: *Charlyce Jones-Owen*
Editor in Chief: *Leah Jewell*
Editorial Assistant: *Patricia Castiglione*
Managing Editor: *Bonnie Biller*
Production Liaison: *Fran Russello*
Editorial/Production Supervision: *Kim Gueterman*
Prepress and Manufacturing Buyer: *Mary Ann Gloriande*
Cover Director: *Jayne Conte*
Cover Art: "Computer Reading" by *Teofilo Olivieri*
Copyeditor: *Kathryn Beck*

This book was set in 10/12 Times Roman by Automated Composition Service
and was printed and bound by RR Donnelley & Sons Company.
The cover was printed by Phoenix Color Corp.

© 1999 by Prentice-Hall, Inc.
Simon & Schuster / A Viacom Company
Upper Saddle River, New Jersey 07458

Printed in the United States of America
10  9  8  7  6  5

ISBN   0-13-633058-4

Prentice-Hall International (UK) Limited, *London*
Prentice-Hall of Australia Pty. Limited, *Sydney*
Prentice-Hall Canada Inc., *Toronto*
Prentice-Hall Hispanoamericana, S.A., *Mexico*
Prentice-Hall of India Private Limited, *New Delhi*
Prentice-Hall of Japan, Inc., *Tokyo*
Simon & Schuster Asia Pte. Ltd., *Singapore*
Editora Prentice-Hall do Brasil, Ltda., *Rio de Janeiro*

For
My
Family

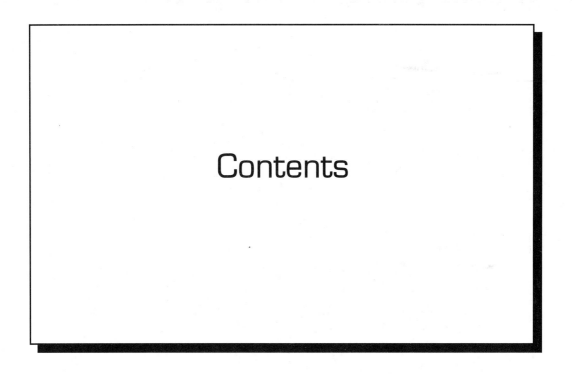

# Contents

## 3    Organizational Strategies    36

# 4   Writing Strategies   47

# 5   Working with Sources   55

# 8   Improving Your Style   91

# 9   Revising Your Writing   101

## 10   Mechanics in Writing with Sources   115

## 11   Sample Student Papers   120

## 12   APA Documentation Style   140

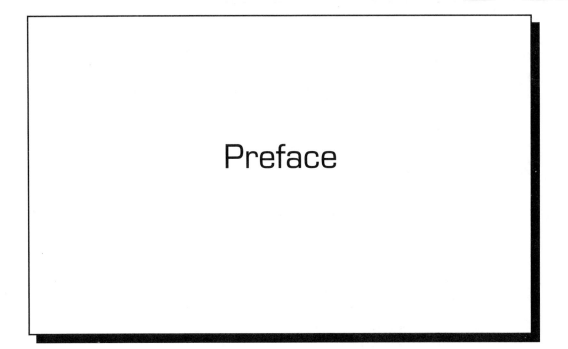

# Preface

During my years of teaching freshman English, I have directed countless research writing assignments, working with students whose efforts ranged from meager and ill directed to those who were academic superstars. When I was Director of Composition at York College of Pennsylvania, I worked with many highly qualified and highly motivated instructors, the "in the trenches" professionals who wanted to assist student researchers but who needed a basic research guide for classroom instruction. This is my attempt to provide a solid "how-to" book for the student research writer. Quite simply, my purpose is to present a practical guide that college students will understand and use, a resource that will help students become better researchers and writers, and that instructors can use in the classroom with ease and confidence.

The style of this book is unique. I address the reader in a direct, informal tone, offering clear explanations and interesting examples of how to use source information. The content is presented in a manner designed to get students to think about the research writing process. The case studies help students see this process from the instructor's perspective as well as give students insights into the writing of other students.

Not only does the style of *Research Writing* promote thinking, it also promotes action. The examples are based on relevant high-interest topics, offering students the opportunity to develop the sample topics.

## ACKNOWLEDGMENTS

I would like to acknowledge the contributions of the following reviewers who provided valuable advice:

- Jane Tainow Feder of New York City Technical College
- Susan A. Nash of Capital University
- Barbara Manrique of California State University, Stanislaus
- Shirley Hart Berry of Cape Fear Community College
- Judith E. Funston of the State University of New York at Potsdam
- Gary Hatch of Bringham Young University
- Mark L. Amdahl of Montgomery County Community College
- Dinty W. Moore of Penn State Altoona
- Frank D. Walters of Auburn University
- John Schaffer of Blinn College
- Marion Van Nostrand of Northeastern University
- James C. McDonald of the University of Southwestern Louisiana
- Christopher Gould of the University of North Carolina at Wilmington
- Patricia E. Connors of the University of Memphis

I appreciate the efforts of Kim Gueterman, my production editor, and Kathryn Beck, my copy editor, as well as the work of Leah Jewell and Patricia Castiglione of Prentice Hall, who kept the project moving.

This text would not have been possible without the encouragement of Dr. Edward T. Jones and the Freshman Composition faculty of York College of Pennsylvania. These dedicated professionals supported my work; I appreciate their encouragement and friendship.

A special thanks goes to Dianne Davis, who assisted with the research, and to Rob Benson and Stephanie Goodermuth Lookenbill, who provided sample essays. I also would like to recognize those students whose interests and struggles inspired me to write this book.

Finally, I must acknowledge the patience and concern shown by my family day after day, month after month while I was involved in the process of researching, writing, and revising. To Melissa and Andrea, my daughters, thanks for understanding me and my work.

**Nancy L. Joseph**
Director, Academic Skills Center
Oakland University

# Introduction

Trudge to the library. Scan the faded pages of dusty reference books. Search for sources that are either outdated or unavailable. Scratch incoherent notes onto stacks of disorganized notecards. Pound the old typewriter through hours and hours of frustration with only fleeting moments of brilliance. And sweat and swear until the whole mess comes together. Ugh! That's the traditional picture of college research writing.

College research in the 1990s, however, differs from the tedious "search and destroy" mission of yesterday. Because computers are able to locate and retrieve information, today's students benefit from a wealth of easily accessible, readily available resources. The computer organizes and stores information as well as accesses hidden files, effortlessly making source information available for your paper. In addition, word processors efficiently produce rough drafts, revised copies, and impressive looking final papers.

The challenge, of course, is for the student researcher to evaluate the sources appropriately and to use them accurately and effectively. Even though today's students enjoy computerized searches and efficient word processors, preparing a research paper remains a difficult process, one that demands a clear focus, a motivated researcher, and lots of time and effort.

Many students are technologically literate, yet they need guidance in locating, evaluating, and incorporating material from electronic sources. Although computers have streamlined research writing, students still have to mastermind the project, a process requiring higher-level critical thinking, synthesizing, and composing abilities. In addition to developing competence with electronic sources, students must understand some basics of research writing: it does not always move along in an organized, linear manner. The truth is that the process may yield many dead ends, requiring students to refocus the research or to select a different topic. These realities of research writing are acknowledged in the explanations presented in this manual.

This research guide encourages students to move beyond the hunt-copy-plagiarize approach typical in much high school research into the realm of college level thinking and writing. It recognizes that students must prepare for the working world by developing the ability to focus, analyze, organize, and compose. This unique approach acknowledges that although college research writing is an academic task, the process reinforces the thinking and writing skills that are essential for success in today's workplace.

Students can eliminate frustration and produce better results by following this current, user-friendly guide to research writing. This manual serves as the student's comprehensive guide to efficient research strategies and current documentation styles for both traditional and electronic sources. While providing the necessary support through direct explanations and clear examples, it challenges students to become curious, self-motivated researchers and recognizes the importance of developing lifelong information-processing skills.

This research guide views the student as an independent researcher, one who must apply the skills learned in Freshman English to papers written in all academic disciplines. In this manner, the emphasis is on research writing as a problem-solving exercise, a practical approach to finding solutions to real-life issues.

This manual is unique because it presents a thorough overview of both traditional and online materials, providing explanations and examples which illustrate the use and documentation of these sources. The emphasis throughout this text is on the Modern Language Association (MLA) documentation style. As a supplement, however, Chapter 12 presents a thorough explanation of American Psychological Association (APA) documentation. A sample research report documented in APA style is included.

## OBJECTIVES

In addition to serving as a guidebook for research writing in Freshman English, this manual is designed to serve as a practical guide to research writing throughout a student's college career. The strategies and materials in this manual are designed to encourage student writers to achieve the following objectives:

- Generate new thoughts and develop new methods for viewing research writing as a means of locating information to solve a problem.
- Understand the process of research writing, focusing on the fact that using information from sources requires time and effort and is full of frustrations, challenges, and rewards.
- Develop the reading, writing, thinking, and researching skills needed for academic as well as for career success, recognizing that searching for information and producing a written product are essential elements in today's workplace.

- View research writing as a problem-solving challenge, one which allows them to apply their research and writing skills to assignments in all academic disciplines.
- Employ a variety of sources ranging from general materials to scholarly articles, going beyond the traditional print resources into nonprint sources such as interviews, surveys, and electronic information.
- Apply active reading techniques as well as effective note taking and organizational skills when gathering information from sources.
- Explore electronic sources and make informed decisions about their use in college research.
- Practice the skills of argument writing by analyzing established beliefs and going beyond accepted pro/con positions into the world of new knowledge and creative problem solving.
- Develop critical thinking skills by viewing research writing as the process of formulating questions and constructing answers.
- Recognize that the research writing process involves planning, organizing, and revising as well as the motivation to formulate questions and to search for answers.
- Become more aware of the strengths and weaknesses of their individual learning styles, thus attempting to develop effective and efficient work habits.
- Understand the importance of accurate documentation of sources and employ source information effectively by reviewing the basics of summarizing, paraphrasing, and quoting.

## OVERVIEW

Chapters 1 and 2 present an introduction, advising the student writer to become aware of the realities of research writing. Chapter 3 reviews organizational strategies and guides the student through the process of selecting sources and focusing a topic. Guidelines for paragraph development are presented in Chapter 4, while Chapter 5 discusses paraphrasing, summarizing, and quoting source material. Chapters 6, 7, and 8 explore the specifics of documentation and the preparation of a works cited list including traditional, electronic, and nonprint sources. The elements of revision, including guidelines for efficient proofreading, are covered in Chapter 9, and Chapter 10 contains material on the mechanics of writing with sources. Two sample student papers, complete with annotations, are included in Chapter 11. Chapter 12 presents an explanation of APA documentation including a sample paper.

# CHAPTER 1

# The Realities
# of
# Research Writing

## SOME BACKGROUND INFORMATION

Before we get into the specifics of preparing a research paper, let's think about some of the realities of research writing. Of course, as a college student you know that research papers are designed to encourage independent reading and writing, challenging you to go beyond the course content into higher levels of thinking and problem solving. And, your instructors have told you that these projects prepare you for workplace writing by requiring you to locate, analyze, and synthesize information. The truth, however, is that many students have some other thoughts about research writing, focusing more on the stress of preparing such a paper than on what they can learn from the experience. Here are some realities to acknowledge as you begin the journey into research writing:

***Research writing takes a lot of time.*** There's no denying that writing a research paper is a time-consuming process. In fact, informal studies of students' work habits reveal that a well-prepared research paper requires approximately forty hours of dedicated effort. Isn't this why your instructor advises you not to wait until the last minute?

What you need to recognize, however, is that the step-by-step completion of the paper and the managing of your time is part of the whole process. In fact, instructors know that the time-management skills you develop as you go through the research and writing process are good preparation for the tasks you will face after graduation in the world of work. Now, that's a reality you can't dispute.

STUDENT'S VIEW

Although I'm a very good student, I have lots of worries when it comes to writing research papers. My usual pattern is to become nervous about my topic once I have started the research. I know that I'll never get an "A" unless I start with a good topic and a strong thesis, so I start second-guessing myself until I lose confidence in my ability to review my own work. After becoming frustrated and worried, I realize that I have to make an appointment to discuss my questions with the professor. Most of the time that really helps. Once a professor told me to figure it out myself, so I talked to a reference librarian who gave me some good advice. There's another problem, though, after I have done the paper and earned a good grade. At times, other students make comments about my good grades because they think that writing research papers is easy for me. They don't believe me when I explain that I write four or five complete drafts before I finish a paper and that I revise my paper for hours and hours over a period of several days. They think that research writing is some type of natural talent, but I know that's not true.

***Research writing may cause frustration.***    Yes, this is another reality that college students face when the instructor announces a research writing assignment. Just getting started causes concern for most students because the scope of the project seems huge, almost unmanageable at times. In the same respect, the focus of the paper seems vague, genuinely foggy for much of the research process. Students seem frustrated because they don't know how to get started; they aren't sure of the questions to ask.

In addition to the scope and focus problems, other questions surface: Is this topic too narrow? Are sources available? Should this paper present my opinion on the topic? How do I document this source? Is it OK to use "I" in my paper?

## AN INQUIRY PROCESS

Students may become frustrated because research writing requires thinking and planning; all of the answers are not readily available in an easy-to-find, easy-to-read format. The solutions are found through a trial-and-error approach, one that requires the research writer to be curious about the topic and to make lots of decisions along the way.

Researching is the process of inquiry. This means that you are looking for solutions to a research question and will discover answers as you move through the process. Some students, however, expect to start with the answer, believing that their job is to place related facts into neat paragraphs to form a complete paper. Sorry, but that approach won't work. A good research paper requires *thinking* as well as time and effort. And, yes, digging for information can be frustrating at times, but that's part of the research writing process.

STUDENT'S VIEW

Writing a research paper can be a real pain because it requires so much time outside of class. When I do put some time into a paper, I'm not always sure that I'm doing the right thing. I get stressed out when my research takes forever or when I have to make several trips to the library to find decent information. Another problem is that my writing seems confusing at times because I'm not sure what I'm trying to say. But I guess that the whole process of putting a paper together isn't too bad. It's been worthwhile because I've developed some good strategies for getting the work done, especially when I start early and stay on the right track. I guess there's a sense of accomplishment when I complete a research paper. I want to celebrate—to party—but soon there's another one to write!

## ANALYZING YOUR STYLE

Before you start your paper, take the time to ask yourself two important questions: What problems do I encounter when preparing a research paper? What strengths do I exhibit when preparing the paper? Answering these questions helps you to improve your approach to research writing.

Take the time to make a list of the difficulties you may have encountered and the strengths you may have exhibited in the past when working on a research paper. The following sample shows one student's analysis:

| **PROBLEMS** | **STRENGTHS** |
| --- | --- |
| Wait too long to get started Procrastination!! | Interested in many topics and willing to research any aspect of topic |
| Too many distractions when writing; many interruptions | Receptive to suggestions for improving paper |
| Focus of paper is confusing; hard to follow a main point | Very willing to revise until paper is OK because concerned about grade |

When you review your research writing strategies, you are attempting to analyze your learning style and to correct your weaknesses. You are trying to avoid problems by developing methods for being more efficient and effective. For example, if you tend to lose the focus of your paper when you are writing the first draft, you may want to do more preliminary work and planning before you start writing. Preparing an organized plan and following it closely may be the solution. To eliminate weaknesses, you should pay attention to your instructor's advice and follow the suggestions presented in this book.

This exercise in analyzing your style also asks you to review your strengths as a student research writer. Being aware of these positive qualities will pull you through if you become frustrated or confused during your work.

You should know that research writing presents two common problems: time management and organization. Are there ways to avoid these problems? Although you can't eliminate these difficulties entirely, you can reduce some of the stress by taking a positive approach to research writing. Consider these points:

**1.   Develop effective research writing skills.** Use techniques that are productive, and eliminate the inefficient practices that produce poor results. For example, if you have a system for taking notes that is more efficient than using note cards, use your approach. If your technique causes confusion, such as with the documentation of sources, it's best to learn a more effective method.

As you move from assignments for your composition course into papers for all academic disciplines, remember that college writing requires a level of independent thinking and dedicated effort that goes beyond what was expected in high school. So give yourself credit for what you know, but be open to suggestions for improving your methods.

**2.   Approach research writing seriously.** There's much to be learned about your topic, and the research writing process provides valuable experiences that are an essential in college as well as in the workplace. That is, the research strategies, analytical thinking abilities, and writing skills developed in college are used in most career fields.

To be more concerned about immediate results, though, remember that a research paper often accounts for a considerable part of your course grade. Isn't that a good reason for taking a serious approach to the paper? And, of course, that's the motivation for allocating an appropriate amount of time to the project.

**3.   View the assignment from the instructor's perspective.** Think about what instructors are looking for when they read students' research assignments by asking yourself some questions: What is the purpose of the assignment? How much time and effort does the instructor expect? How will my work be evaluated? These issues are worth your consideration because if you can see the assignment from the instructor's point of view, you will have a better idea of how to present your information.

**4.   Manage your time effectively.** Set a timetable for preparing the paper and stick to it, allocating plenty of time to make changes and to revise your work. Remember that a good research paper develops through continued effort over a period of time, not through a last-minute rush of adrenaline and late-night sessions on the word processor.

The first step is to get started early because research paper disasters (such as an uncooperative word processor or a hard to find reference source) may occur. Although most students have good intentions, many delay because they're not sure where to start. Don't make excuses about not understanding the assignment because procrastinating only makes you feel more frustrated about the work that needs to be done.

---

STUDENT'S VIEW

Why do I wait until the last minute when doing a research paper? Well, I always have other assignments that take up my time. Besides, I can't really get into a topic until I feel the pressure of the due date, and then I work through the night to finish the paper. My grades? They're about average. Maybe they could be better.

---

Here's a good way to begin: Write down three possible topics and three approaches to each. Select a topic and one approach and start your preliminary reading and thinking. If this leads to a dead end, select another approach for the same topic or choose a different topic. The point is that you won't know if your ideas will work until you try to develop them. (Focusing the topic and clustering are discussed in Chapter 2.) Another reason to start early is to avoid the frenzied rush for library resources which always occurs before a paper is due.

   **5.   Use resources wisely.** Your resources, of course, are not just limited to print sources from the college library. Successful students learn that resources include everything from the services of the reference librarian to a variety of computerized and nonprint sources. Using resources wisely also means asking your instructor for advice because this is the person who best understands what you have to do to prepare a successful paper. And, very importantly, this is the person who grades the paper!

## SEEKING CLARIFICATION OR EXPECTING TOO MUCH HELP?

Most college students don't take advantage of their instructor's expertise and therefore do a great disservice to themselves by guessing what an assignment requires. It only makes sense, however, to save the time and frustration by asking questions to be certain that you understand the assignment. How can you meet the requirements of the assignment if you don't understand the instructor's expectations?

   To understand the requirements for a research paper, you must pay attention in class when the assignment is discussed. In addition, you should review the assignment sheet the instructor distributes, ask questions in class, and listen to the concerns that other students express.

   If you need additional clarification, make an appointment to stop by the instructor's office. Have some questions ready and show the instructor some of your work, maybe a list of possible topics, a tentative outline, or a few sample paragraphs. If you walk in with a blank tablet and no preliminary work, it's evident that you expect the instructor to tell you the answers while you sit in the office taking dictation. Many instructors are uncomfortable with this approach, recognizing that some students become too dependent because they may lack the confidence or the motivation to do the work themselves.

The best approach is to get something started, and then make an appointment with the instructor to discuss your concerns. Take the time to review your work before your meeting so that it's fresh in your mind. Bring a list of questions to the conference. This strategy is effective because it shows that you are able to evaluate your own work, and that you are not expecting the instructor to do the thinking for you. Many students use the services of the campus writing center at this stage of the writing process.

## REVIEWING THE STEPS IN RESEARCH WRITING

Research writing doesn't always progress in a step-by-step manner, but the following list presents a general overview of the process:

1. Understand the assignment and determine a time schedule
2. Select a topic
3. Conduct some preliminary research; get some background information
4. Review your topic; be sure that it meets the requirements of the assignment
5. Formulate a preliminary thesis and identify the focus of your paper
6. Research the topic, remembering to evaluate the reliability of your sources
7. Organize your ideas by limiting the topic and revising the thesis
8. Develop a supporting argument by locating appropriate sources
9. Devise a plan for the paper by outlining or listing your ideas
10. Write a first draft of your paper
11. Revise the draft; check your focus and your argument
12. Rewrite weak areas; locate more source information if necessary
13. Write a second draft incorporating strategies for revision
14. Proofread your paper
15. Prepare the final copy.

---

INSTRUCTOR'S VIEW

I have started using the process approach to writing in my courses. When I assign papers in Principles of Marketing, I arrange a date to review the students' outlines and the first drafts of the papers. Even though this technique takes time, it results in better papers because I can advise students about their work before they turn in the final copy. If a problem is evident in the outline, I can offer suggestions for strengthening the paper. Another advantage is that this approach keeps the students from waiting until the last minute to begin their work. I do not require students to turn in drafts for my review, but the papers I do critique seem to earn higher grades. I wish more students would ask for a preliminary reading.

### Some Reminders

- Develop productive, efficient writing strategies by taking the time to analyze your approach. Think about your strengths and weaknesses as a research writer.
- Manage your time wisely. Avoid excuses and last minute frustrations by getting started early and by maintaining a realistic time schedule.
- Recognize that the writing process does not always move in a step-by-step manner.

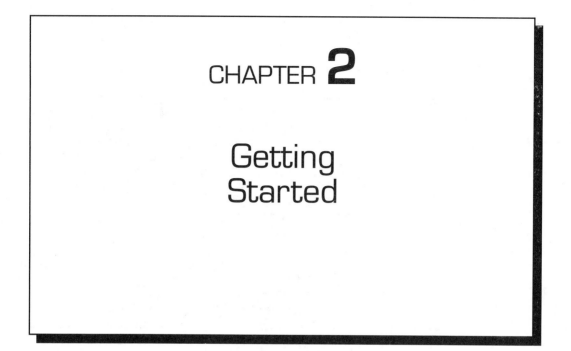

CHAPTER **2**

# Getting
# Started

## UNDERSTANDING THE ASSIGNMENT

Make sure that you understand the assignment. Contrary to what some college students believe, a research paper does more than present a collection of facts. As the author of the paper, you need to do something with the facts. This means that you need to understand the purpose of the assignment and arrange the material according to the specific requirements. For example, if you are writing a paper on labor unions, how will you approach the topic? Consider these options:

**Compare/Contrast:** How are American labor unions different from unions in other countries? How are they similar to unions in other countries? How is a unionized workplace different from a nonunion workplace? How are they alike? How are American unions in the 1990s different from unions in the 1940s?

**Pro/Con:** Present arguments to support the existence of labor unions. Present arguments to support the elimination of labor unions.

**Problem/Solution:** Explore the problems associated with America's labor unions and propose solutions. Explore problems in the workplace that led to the formation of labor unions.

**Causal Analysis:** Explain the causes of the decline of labor unions. Analyze the reasons labor unions should exist in today's workplace by examining the pros and cons of each point and by presenting a conclusion.

**Exposition:** Explain the facts about labor unions. Examine the role unions play in the workplace today.

INSTRUCTOR'S VIEW

The research paper for my advanced Political Thought course requires students to ex-amine the present jury system in the United States. Students are told to take a position that advocates supporting or abolishing the jury system; they must present evidence from sources to back up their position. The requirements are explained in class and are accompanied by a written assignment sheet. Every semester I have one or two students who don't follow the directions. One paper presented a carefully researched history of the jury system, but it received a low grade because it didn't address the required issues—it didn't take a position on the system. I wish students would pay attention to the specifics of the assignment.

Meeting the research requirements means that you must understand the assign-ment. Most instructors specify the number and types of sources, but if this informa-tion is not presented to you, ask some questions. How many sources should be used? Does the paper require primary research such as a survey or questionnaire that you construct? Should your research be limited to scholarly sources or are general sources such as *Newsweek* or *U.S. News & World Report* acceptable? Are books good sources of information for your topic, or should you use articles from periodicals? Does your instructor approve of online sources which are available through the Internet? Should you go beyond the print sources into original materials such as interviews and per-sonal observations? Once you understand the research requirements for your paper, you are ready to select a topic.

## RESEARCH WRITING AND ARGUMENTATION

Research writing may involve exposition or argumentation. An expository paper re-quires the explanation and analysis of a topic, whereas an argumentative paper re-quires that a thesis be supported by evidence in a logical, unemotional manner. In many cases, however, research writing requires you to combine both strategies be-cause you may be asked to first explain your topic and then present a position sup-ported by evidence. Be certain to understand the focus your instructor requires.

**Exposition**
**Explain and analyze a topic**

Sample: Discuss the Treaty of Versailles and explain the position of the Allies. Analyze the impact of the treaty on Germany.

**Argumentation**
**Take a position and support it with evidence**

Sample: The conditions of the Treaty of Versailles gave Germany the impetus for starting World War II.

**Exposition and argumentation**
**Present an explanation and take a position**

Sample: Explain the conditions of the Treaty of Versailles and argue that it gave Germany the impetus for starting World War II.

Effective argumentation requires you to narrow a topic, take a position, analyze the evidence, respond to your reader's concerns, and present a strong conclusion. Most college papers involve argumentation because instructors want students to become familiar with topics by taking a position and by presenting evidence to support or refute a main premise. Through argumentation you are able to explore an issue, present a new point of view, and recommend a solution.

The process of argumentation involves three phases: inquiry, analysis, and persuasion. Review these explanations:

**Inquiry:** Ask questions and seek information so you will understand your topic. Inquiry enables you to formulate a position and find supporting evidence.
**Analysis:** Critically review your position and determine how to present your evidence. Analysis involves thinking about the logical support of your position.
**Persuasion:** Convince your readers to accept your position. Your credibility as a research writer and your ability to analyze your audience are major factors in persuasion.

## AUDIENCE ANALYSIS

Research writing requires you to analyze your audience. This means that you have to think about the needs of your readers as you are researching and writing. (Unless your instructor indicates otherwise, you can assume that your readers are a group of your peers.) Consider the following questions:

**Who is my audience?**
Will my readers be interested in my topic?
How much knowledge of the topic will they have?

**How can I persuade my audience to accept my thesis?**
Will my evidence be persuasive?
How should I present my explanations so the reader will understand?

Using an appropriate style is another element of connecting with your audience. You should "talk" to your readers as you offer examples and explanations. Anticipate your readers' responses and answer their objections, being certain that you leave no unanswered questions. Your language should not be formal and elevated, nor should it be informal and careless. Your wording should be planned and deliberate, but not stiff and pompous. Reading your work aloud will help you judge the appropriateness of your style. As a general guideline, limit your use of "I" and "you." Do not use contractions or other forms of informal wording. (Refer to "Revising the Wording of Your Paper" in Chapter 9.)

INSTRUCTOR'S VIEW

I like to guide students when they are writing research papers for my courses, but I'm not comfortable with the students who want too much assistance, the ones who seem lost and helpless when they come to my office for help. When I say "too much assistance," I mean the student who must check with me every step of the way or the one who expects me to write down the ideas for the paper. Sometimes I feel that this student is looking for a good grade by having me do the thinking that is required for research writing. This is unfair to the other students who are doing their own work.

Talk with your instructor to determine the point of view, or *voice*, required for your research paper. Many instructors provide sample papers demonstrating the required style. For all research writing, however, the goal is to limit personal references and to avoid awkward, distracting wording.

For some research writing assignments, using subjective statements with the pronoun "I" is acceptable. A good example of the effective use of "I" in research writing appears in "The Threat of Affirmative Action," a student paper located in Chapter 11. In this paper, the student writer includes a brief paragraph presenting his own experiences with affirmative action. This personal experience adds strength to the writer's position, demonstrating to the reader that he has experience beyond the information found in his print sources. His credibility as a research writer is enhanced through the use of this personal example because it is concisely presented and directly related to the thesis. Note that this paragraph is the only section of the paper using subjective "I" statements.

## SELECTING A TOPIC

Some instructors assign topics or restrict students to a general area of study, whereas others allow students free choice. Remember the advantage of assigned topics—you can get started with the research without having to spend time finding a topic. Regardless of your instructor's approach, your job is to identify and narrow a suitable topic for your research paper, being certain that the topic meets the requirements of the assignment.

The best advice is to follow your instructor's suggestions when selecting a topic. If the instructor doesn't offer suggested topics, ask for a few ideas because the instructor knows which topics will work well and which to avoid. Another approach is to prepare a list of three topics and your reasons for selecting each. Ask your instructor to review your list and to offer suggestions for making the final decision.

When selecting a topic, consider your interests and your personal experiences.

Many students prefer to work on topics that relate to their majors because this provides a broader understanding of their career fields. Other students prefer contemporary issues because they want to become better informed about current events. Here are some factors to consider when selecting a topic:

1. Make sure that your topic is suitable for the assignment. If your topic doesn't meet the requirements, you will have a difficult time producing an acceptable paper.
2. Source material must be available. If the topic is too current, source material will be limited. At times, only news reports, not the detailed analysis of the topic, are available for current issues.
3. The topic must present an issue, allowing you to develop a specific position and to support it.
4. The topic must be suitable for college research. If it lacks scholarly content, select another topic.
5. Don't choose the first topic that comes to mind. Take the time to think about your choice.

Once you have selected a topic and started the research, stay with that idea. Avoid changing topics unless you have a valid reason such as the fact that your topic doesn't fit the requirements of the assignment. Students often waste time by the needless, last-minute changing of topics. Remember that if you make a change, the second choice may be just as frustrating as the first topic. The best advice is to select a topic carefully so that your effort goes into producing a good paper, not into worrying about the topic.

**TOPICS TO AVOID**

**Some topics are trendy and overused**
   Steroids and Athletics
   Date Rape
**Some topics are too emotionally charged**
   Abortion Rights
   Death Penalty
**Some topics are too broad**
   Environmental Problems
   Violence on Television
   The Rise and Fall of Nazi Germany
**Some topics are boring**
   Why We Need Fresh Drinking Water
   Grooming Your Pet
**Some personal experience topics can't be supported by library research**
   The Fulfillment I Experience through Working with Children
   The Joy of Traveling in Canada

Allow plenty of time to think about your topic because it must keep your interest throughout the lengthy process of researching, writing, and rewriting. This is why it's important to do as much preliminary reading as possible, giving yourself a good idea of the issues you will be working with as you prepare your research paper.

INSTRUCTOR'S VIEW

What are the common problems students face when selecting a topic for a research paper? From my experience I know that students make a mistake when they choose a trendy topic, such as saving the rain forests, because it is so common that no one is interested in reading about it. Topics that produce lists of information and examples but do not leave room for much original thought are also problematic. For example, when students write papers on the dangers of drug abuse, they often copy lots of facts from sources and add an emotional story or two to fill up the paper. They fail to take a position, so the paper shows little thought. If a student wants to write about drug use, a better paper would be an argument either for or against the legalization of drugs. Even though that topic is used frequently, it does require some thinking and that's what I'm looking for in students' papers. There's plenty of solid evidence to support either side of the legalization issue.

## USING A COLLEGE LIBRARY

Become familiar with your college library before you begin your research. Most college writing courses include an introduction to the library complete with informative materials and a tour, providing you with a valuable opportunity to learn about the facility where you will be spending hours and hours during your college years.

It's important to remember that research for your college papers should be done in a college or university library rather than in a community library. In most communities, the public library is designed to provide nonacademic information to the general population, whereas a college library is designed to provide scholarly sources for academic research.

In order to work efficiently and effectively, you will need to learn as much as possible about your college library. Be certain to focus on the following elements as you become familiar with the library:

> Circulation Desk
> Card Catalog or Public Access Catalog (PAC)
> General Reference Sources
> Specialized Reference Sources
> Periodical Indexes
> Government Documents
> Audio-Visual Sources

For some students, searching for source material may seem tedious and unproductive at times. You may become frustrated when you learn that several good sources are unavailable or will not work with your thesis. Remember, however, that the research process is a vital part of your college experience because it gives you the opportunity to develop problem-solving skills and to strengthen your analytical thinking abilities. These skills go beyond your writing course, extending into your other college courses and into your career field.

Most research strategies follow this pattern:

1. Identify a topic and review some general sources to get an overview of the available information
2. Focus and refine the topic and locate preliminary sources
3. Narrow the topic and locate appropriate sources
4. Take notes and build a working bibliography.

## USING LIBRARY SOURCES TO SELECT A TOPIC

You may want to conduct an online search to help you locate a topic. This can be done by using the Internet to search for information. Select a search tool that provides a subject directory and then select a category. You will move through a series of menus until you arrive at a suitable Web site. Many students find that a subject directory search tool such as the Internet Services List (available at http://www.spectracom.com/islist) provides an easy approach to topic selection.

The library's Public Access Catalog (PAC) provides a convenient way to find and narrow a topic. This computerized card catalog allows researchers to locate materials related to the narrowed topic. Follow these steps for using the PAC:

- Begin with a broad subject
- Review the subtopics
- Select a subtopic
- Preview the list of sources
- Select appropriate sources and print out a list.

If you are having trouble selecting a topic, you may want to use a series of books titled *Opposing Viewpoints*. Most college libraries have this series in CD-ROM format, which can be accessed through a title search in a computerized card catalog. This series is helpful because it contains seventy books, each on a topic suitable for college research. Each book presents a number of pro-and-con articles as well as a complete bibliography. *Opposing Viewpoints* is a good *starting point* for research writing because it allows you to review many topics and sources in a short time. Once you have selected a topic and previewed several articles, you can use the bibliography to conduct a thorough search for additional sources. Remember, however, that your research must go beyond the articles in *Opposing Viewpoints* and into a variety of sources.

Another way to locate a topic is to review the periodical indexes for the subject area of your interest. For example, the *Business Periodicals Index*, which is available online through First Search, lists hundreds of business periodicals. If you skim through the list of articles, you may find topics that interest you. In the same respect,

*Legal Trac*, a CD-ROM through *INFO-Trac*, presents topics related to law and legal proceedings.

Some resources available in print form are the *Library of Congress Subject Headings* and the *Propaedia to the New Encyclopedia Britannica.* These reference books list hundreds of subjects suitable for college research writing. Of course, a reference librarian can assist you in using these resources and in selecting a research topic.

## Library of Congress Subject Headings

Available in the reference section of the library, the *Library of Congress Subject Headings* is a multivolume catalog that lists only subject headings. This resource provides a good starting point for your research because it helps you identify a topic as well as narrow it by using subject categories. Most college libraries have the *Library of Congress Subject Headings* available in the traditional print form as well as in the updated electronic form.

Once you understand how to locate headings and key words, your research process will become easier. The following sample of subjects is taken from the *Library of Congress Subject Headings:*

**College**
College costs
[LB2342]
College education costs
Student expenditures
Tuition
Education—Finance
Student aid
Student loan funds
Student tax credits
College credits
Outside work
Grading and marking
Student activities
College degrees
USE Degrees, academic
College departmental libraries
College desegregation
USE College integration
College discipline (*May Subd Geog*)
University discipline
School discipline
Self-government
College drama
College dropouts
College attendance
Dropouts
College employees
College enrollment

College entrance
Achievement tests
Subject specialty tests
Educational measurement
Prediction of success
Advanced placement
College Entrance Examination
English Composition Test
College Entrance Requirements
subdivision under names of
universities & colleges,
e.g., Harvard University
College environment
College etiquette
College facilities
(*May Subd Geog*)
Community use
Extended use of
Planning
Campus planning
College faculty
USE College Teachers
College Fraternities
USE Greek Letter societies
College freshman
(*May Subd Geog*)
SA subdivision Freshmen under
names of university, etc.

The online *Library of Congress Subject Headings* provides an extensive list of subject directories on the Internet at this address: http://lcweb.loc.gov.

Although periodical indexes are found in the traditional paper copies, some are available in a database which allows you to conduct quick, efficient searches. The databases, however, are limited to the past five or ten years, while the paper copies may extend back one hundred years. (For a list of paper and electronic indexes, refer to Appendix A.)

## DOING SOME EXPLORATORY READING

Your preliminary work should include reading some general reference materials such as books and encyclopedias to get an idea of the scope of your topic. This is important because you want to learn as much as possible in the early stages of the research process so you can avoid problems as you work on your paper. Remember that research is the process of discovery. This means that you are trying to educate yourself about the topic. Some student researchers see this early stage as the time to collect a pile of sources so they can meet the quota established by the instructor. These students become so involved in accumulating material that they fail to select the sources carefully and to take the time to explore the topic in a meaningful manner. The result is a weak paper because it is based on a poor selection of sources.

Taking the time to do some exploratory reading, however, will allow you to become aware of the various issues related to your topic. It will reveal if an adequate number of current, relevant sources is available.

General encyclopedias, such as *Encyclopaedia Britannica and Encyclopedia Americana*, provide good background information that will guide you as you search for other sources. They serve as a valuable starting point when compiling a working bibliography. Many professors discourage students from using these sources in college papers because they prefer more scholarly materials; however, these sources are useful when you are beginning to explore your topic.

For more specific information, ask a reference librarian to direct you to specialized sources. Here is a listing of some specialized encyclopedias, dictionaries, and other reference books:

> *International Encyclopedia of Communications*
> *International Directory of Company Histories*
> *International Encyclopedia of the Social Sciences*
> *Encyclopaedia of Black America*
> *Encyclopedia of Crime and Justice*
> *Encyclopedia of American Facts and Dates*
> *Encyclopedia of Southern Culture*
> *Encyclopedia of World Art*
> *Encyclopedia of Bioethics*
> *Encyclopedia of Legal Information Sources*

STUDENT'S VIEW

I have a hard time with directions for assignments because I'm not always sure where to start or what to write, so I learned a new method. I get the paper started and then take it to the instructor for advice. The instructors are very willing to give me suggestions about using better sources and about organizing the information. One problem, though, is that it takes me twice as long to research and write a paper because I'm not using the old shortcuts I depended on to write a paper. After two years of low grades, I decided to get some help with my work, even if it means rewriting the paper. Yes, my grades have improved, but I have to spend more time on each assignment.

*McGraw-Hill Encyclopedia of Science and Technology*
*Black's Law Dictionary*
*Black's Medical Dictionary*
*Cambridge World History of Human Disease*
*Dictionary of the Middle Ages*
*Dictionary of Contemporary American Artists*
*Dictionary of Biology*
*Dictionary of Computing*
*Dictionary of Business and Management*
*Sourcebook of Hispanic Culture in the United States*
*Columbia Encyclopedia of Nutrition*
*Magill's Survey of Science: Earth Science Series*
*American Educators' Encyclopedia*
*Guide to Multicultural Resources*
*Statistical Abstracts of the United States*
*Basic Statistics of the European Communities*
*Recycling in America: A Reference Handbook*
*Chemical Engineers' Handboook*
*Contemporary Literary Criticism*

A review of relevant material in reference books will provide you with an overview of the topic, which will help you focus your research and develop a preliminary thesis statement.

## FOCUSING THE TOPIC AND CLUSTERING IDEAS

Once you have selected a topic, the next step is to get it focused. Narrowing a general subject into a research topic is an essential step in research writing. Begin this process by reviewing the meaning of these terms:

> *Subject:* general area of study
> *Topic:* specific aspect of the subject

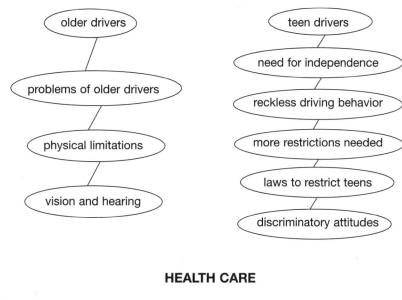

**DRIVING**

older drivers

problems of older drivers

physical limitations

vision and hearing

teen drivers

need for independence

reckless driving behavior

more restrictions needed

laws to restrict teens

discriminatory attitudes

**HEALTH CARE**

| Advancements in Medicine | Organ Donations and Transplants | Experimental Procedures | Medical Malpractice | Cost of Health Care |
|---|---|---|---|---|
| —Cancer Research | —Effectiveness | —Cost | —Legal Issues | —HMO Programs |
| —AIDS Research | —Moral Questions | —Research | —Insurance | —Medicare |
| —Cure for Arthritis | —Locating Donors | —Moral Issues | —High Costs | —Hospital Costs |

As you know, the topic must be limited enough to be developed fully within the confines of your paper. This allows you to explore one aspect of the topic in a complete manner and follow a focused thesis throughout the entire paper.

There are several ways to divide your subject into categories that make good topics for a paper. Use the prewriting strategy of *clustering*, as shown in the above example, to generate ideas. You can start with a general subject and work down to a specific topic.

## USING ELECTRONIC INDEXES TO NARROW A TOPIC

Electronic indexes, which are available in most public and college libraries, are excellent resources for helping the student researcher narrow a topic. The purpose of these CD-ROM systems is to assist you in moving from a broad subject to specific topics and to provide a list of articles from current periodicals on the topic. For example, the general subject of "education" has 127 subdivisions and 90 related subjects in the *INFO-Trac* databases. Here is a survey of the subject headings:

**EDUCATION**

| | |
|---|---|
| Education, Agricultural | Education, Industry |
| Education Alternatives | Education, Liberal |
| Education Amendments | Education of Children |
| Education and Anthropology | Education of Workers |
| Education and Business | Adult Education |
| Education and Crime | Alcohol Education |
| Education and Demography | Alternative Education |
| Education and Sociology | Bilingual Education |
| Education, Character | Career Education |
| Education, Home | Compensatory Education |
| Education, Higher | Cooperative Education |
| Education, Intercultural | Early Childhood Education |
| Education, Medical | Graduate Education |
| Education, Moral | Musical Education |

When using a computerized search, you can easily scan the subtopics and choose one for a narrow search. For example, if you selected the topic of "education of adults" in the *INFO-Trac* database, you would find 173 entries on this topic, with 40 subdivisions and 10 related topics. Using the electronic search, you can scan the titles of the articles and make decisions about which subtopics to pursue because the topic of "education of adults" is too broad.

Here is a listing of sample articles for the topic "education of adults," which will help you narrow this topic. Be careful to look for scholarly sources. Although general sources, such as magazines, provide some interesting background information, do not overuse these types of sources for college research. When using *INFO-Trac* or other general online databases, remember that these resources serve as a starting point for your research.

> Adult-centered classroom: a distinct learning atmosphere for college students. Vince Konicek. Adult Learning, Jan–Feb 1996 v7 n3 p13(3).
> —Abstract Available—
> Helping baby-boomers face the '90s. Jane R. Flagello. Education Digest, Nov 1995 v61 n3 p6(3).
> Work force education: staff development options. Dennis Terdy. Adult Learning, June 1997 v7 n2 p13(2).
> —Abstract Available—
> Adult education in the military: leading the field in innovation. Adult Learning, March–April 1996 v6 n4 p5(1).
> —Abstract Available—
> Back to school. Erick Schonfeld. Fortune, Sept 4, 1995 v 132 n5 p137(1).

When the notation states "Abstract Available," this means that the database contains a brief summary of the article as shown in the following sample:

INSTRUCTOR'S VIEW

As a composition instructor, I have worked with college students' research papers for many years. I have observed that many students create difficulties for themselves because of the way they approach the assignment. The number-one problem is that most students don't do an adequate amount of preliminary work early enough in the semester to get a clear understanding of where they are going with their topics. For example, many students wait weeks before getting started, and then they rush through the essential steps of selecting a topic, doing some background reading, and focusing the paper. Because these students have procrastinated, they are frantic once they get started and madly grab for any source that may or may not relate to their thesis. When they bring in a draft for my review, I discover a mess of unrelated paragraphs, so I try to explain why the content is weak. I offer ideas for strengthening the paper, and most students are able to see the problems and to correct the weaknesses. A few students become agitated because my suggestions indicate that they have more work to do if they want to earn a good grade on the paper.

European lifelong learning initiatives. Bryan T. Peck. Phi Delta Kappan, May 1996 v77 n9 p645(2).
Abstract: Europe is taking steps to encourage lifelong learning for people of any age as a means to help them achieve fulfilling lives at any age. In many European countries, 20–25% of the population will be over age 65 by year 2030.
Subjects: Retirees—Education
Education—Demographic aspects
Continuing education—Europe
Adult education—Europe

After you have narrowed the topic, check the requirements of your assignment to be certain that your plans for the paper will meet the instructor's expectations. Now that you have focused your topic, you are ready to select sources for your paper.

## SELECTING SOURCES

As the writer, your job is to locate and consolidate information from several sources that substantiate your main idea or thesis. The material from the outside sources backs up your views, thus making it possible to create an original paper.

When doing research, consider all available sources: print and nonprint, traditional and nontraditional. Go beyond the usual encyclopedias and books. Using information from surveys, periodicals, interviews, pamphlets, news programs, or government documents often provides the depth required for college-level research papers.

Limit your use of popular, general interest sources (such as *Time*, *Newsweek*, *Psychology Today*, etc.) to your background reading. The content of these sources is general, not scholarly, so you should not base your entire paper on information from this type of source. Information from general sources may be used to supplement the material from scholarly sources. Articles from scholarly journals, by contrast, are reliable and current and should serve as the base of your academic research.

Another guideline to follow when preparing a college research paper is to limit your use of books. Using books may cause you to rely too heavily on an author's conclusions rather than on your own ideas. Many instructors ask students to limit their use of books because the information tends to be dated and more current information can be found in scholarly publications. If you need assistance in selecting appropriate sources, consult a reference librarian and follow the suggestions of your instructor.

When searching for sources, look for information to substantiate the main points you will present in your paper. Avoid choosing source material indiscriminately—selecting sources just because they relate to your topic and not because they support the points you are trying to make. A "hit-or-miss" approach to research results in a pointless, incoherent collection of quotations. Be advised that such a product is not acceptable for a college paper.

### Using Newspapers As Sources

At times you may want to research a current topic, one that is so new that it is covered only in newspapers and in weekly newsmagazines. The best advice is to avoid topics that are too current because the information often is limited to news reports and does not include a detailed analysis and commentary on the topic. If you must write on a current topic, however, use the most authoritative newspapers such as *The New York Times*, the *Wall Street Journal*, or the *Washington Post*. Avoid using your hometown newspaper unless you are writing about local issues.

### Primary and Secondary Sources

Your instructor might require you to use primary sources. A *primary source* is the original source of information on a specific topic. For example, when a research team presents the results of its research in a professional journal, such as in the *Journal of*

---

STUDENT'S VIEW

When a research paper is first assigned, I'm excited about the idea of searching for information. After several trips to the library, though, I become frustrated with what I find. Maybe I don't have a realistic picture of the kinds of sources I should be using, and I do admit that for some papers I have used any old source just to avoid going back to the library. Soon the paper becomes a nightmare because I have lost my enthusiasm. My instructor always says that my topic isn't focused, but I don't know how to fix it. Do you think a reference librarian could help?

*the American Medical Association*, their article is a primary source. Other primary sources are original literary works, interviews, speeches, and personal manuscripts.

Locating primary sources may be difficult, so instructors may allow you to use *secondary sources*, which summarize and interpret information from primary sources. For example, the *Washington Post* may print an article about the research team's work. The information for this article was taken from the primary source, which was a professional journal. The *Washington Post* article, which describes the scientific findings and offers an analysis of what the findings mean, is a secondary source.

Students readily recognize that secondary sources are easier to read and interpret than primary sources. Some instructors, however, prefer primary sources for college research because these sources require you to present your interpretations instead of relying on the views of the author of a secondary source.

Consult with your instructor regarding the use of primary and secondary sources. For additional information, see pages 71–72 of this manual.

## EVALUATING YOUR SOURCES

Once you have located sources that appear suitable for your paper, take the time to evaluate each carefully. A critical look at your materials before you begin writing is important because it gives you the chance to discard inappropriate or irrelevant sources before you have worked them into your paper.

Reviewing your sources also helps you focus your paper and refine your thoughts. Consider the following when evaluating your research sources:

**1.**   Is the source reliable? Was the material published in an academic journal or by a scholarly press such as a university press? Articles published by well-known newspapers and general magazines can be regarded as reliable, but remember to limit your use of these types of sources.

**2.**   Is the author well known in the field? Is the author's name mentioned in other sources? Are the author's credentials listed? Check the bibliographies of reference articles.

**3.**   Does the source present adequate evidence to support the main points? Does the author use facts, expert opinion, statistics, and counterarguments to present a position? Does the author acknowledge the opposing views?

**4.**   Does the source have a balanced tone or is it biased? For example, a publication by the tobacco industry is certain to defend cigarette smoking. If you choose to use such a publication, be certain to recognize that the author's position will not be balanced.

**5.**   Does the author consider the views of other sources? Does it present a fair representation of other authors? Are opposing views recognized?

**6.** Is the source current? Was it published within the past five to seven years? Although the timeliness may be less important in some academic disciplines, it is essential for scientific research. For some topics, the author's credentials may be more important than the publication date.

If you have trouble making decisions about your sources, consult an expert. Often your professor as well as the reference librarian can give advice and offer suggestions for selecting appropriate sources.

## EVALUATING ONLINE SOURCES

As a student researcher, you will discover that thousands of databases are available to you through the World Wide Web (WWW, or Web). These resources range from electronic journals, magazines, newspaper articles, and newsletters to online discussion groups. Creating a new approach to scholarship, computer-based research provides easy access to hundreds of valuable sources.

The key to using electronic resources effectively for college research depends on your careful evaluation of individual sources. This means that you need to consider several factors when selecting online sources for your paper—for example, their permanence and timeliness. You should also try to identify the "publisher" of the information and evaluate the authorship of the source, thereby establishing its reliability.

Documents derived from an online database are divided into two categories:

**1. Material that identifies a specific print source:** This may be a reprint of an article from any print source such as a journal, government document, newspaper, or magazine. These materials are the same as the original, which was initially printed. For example, you may locate an article from *The New York Times* that was originally printed in the newspaper. Remember that the page numbers for the online source will not follow the original numbering.

---

STUDENT'S VIEW

For the paper I'm writing on homeschooling, I searched the Internet for sources. I'm not sure how I found it, but I located a page on one of the Web sites labeled "Why Your Child Should Not Attend School." The author describes why her children are home-schooled, and she tells some interesting stories about public schools, but I couldn't follow her reasoning. Many of her statements seemed emotional and not very logical. I have doubts about some of the "facts" she presents about teachers neglecting students. She identified herself only as "ANON Western USA," so there is no way to check her credibility. I guess that I won't be using this source in my paper.

---

**2.   Material that does not identify a specific print source:** Some online sources, such as electronic bulletin boards and the Internet, provide information on a wide range of topics. You should avoid these informal, nondocumented sources for academic papers because the origin and authorship often are unknown. This means that you may not know if the author of an article such as "Living on the Moon in the 21st Century" is a credible scholar in the field or a prankster who writes science fiction.

## Permanence

The issue of permanence centers around the ability to retrieve the source at any time. Files on the Internet change form regularly as they are edited or even deleted. A file may not reside in a given location from one day to the next because the information may move from server to server. As you can see, this causes problems when the reader of your paper checks the sources you used and discovers that you documented your writing with online sources of questionable origin that were not permanent.

A related issue involves changes in the electronic text itself. Libraries subscribe to databases (such as *Associated Press News*, *Aerospace Database*, and *Forensic Science*), which may be updated several times a year as new entries are added and existing entries are corrected. It is important for you to know if the database you cite in your paper is modified regularly and to cite the version you used accurately.

Your credibility as a researcher declines when your sources cannot be immediately retrieved or are unavailable in the same form you cited. For this reason, most instructors recommend that you use only permanent online documents from recognized publications. Before you begin your research, ask your instructor to specify the types of online sources that are acceptable for your paper.

## Timeliness

Always check the currency (the publication date and the listing of revisions) of your sources. This applies to all sources except historical documents or archives. If you have located a Web site that can be edited, note the dates of the changes. This information may be presented for the entire Web site or may be included with individual files. A document without a date is less reliable than one that has been modified.

## Reliability

Use Internet sources that are well documented and reliable. That is, it is your job as the researcher to determine as much background information as possible about a source and its credibility before you use it in your paper.

To effectively evaluate your online documents, you need to understand some basics of electronic sources. The "server" of online or Internet documents is a computer service that takes requests from computer users and provides access to the informa-

---

### YEAR-ROUND SCHOOLING

### WHY YEAR-ROUND SCHOOLING?

Douglas County is the fastest-growing county in the United States: growth is phenomenal!!! As a result there is a constant need for more schools. New schools cost property owners money, so to cut down this cost the district builds schools that will hold 25% more student capacity than it can hold at one time. On any given school day, 75% of the student body are in session, 25% are on break.

How Does the Year-Round System Work?

Students are divided into four tracks (A, B, C, D). On any given day, three of the tracks are in session and one track is on break. Everyone is on break during Christmas and other holidays. With some variation, students and their track teachers attend school for nine weeks, then get three weeks of break. When students and teachers go on break, their classroom supplies are packed up and placed in storage. The "tracking on" students and teachers move into their classroom. Thus, students and teachers continually swap classrooms.
Coyote Creek is designed around this system. Take a look at our floor plan and you'll see that it is divided into three pods, one pod for each track in session. As we track back on from break we rotate counter clockwise from pod to pod.

Why Is Coyote Creek on a Conventional Calendar This First Year?

Being a new school, Mr. David Ray, our principal, wants the whole staff together for a year. He believes this will get the school off to a better start. However, this desire may be short lived. Our student enrollment has increased beyond projected estimates. The school has become overcrowded and we may be forced to go year-round in January. Time will tell!

---

tion. In some cases it is difficult to determine who provided the information to the server—who is the "publisher." For this reason, the server cannot guarantee the accuracy of the information it provides.

To ascertain the reliability of an online document, first determine if the Web site is official. Note if it is supported by a reputable institution (such as a university or an official government agency) or by an authority in the field. Is a statement of authority or a notice of the source available? Review the site's statement of purpose which appears on the lead page for general information about the scope and philosophy of the site. Check the author's credentials. Has the author's work been published in scholarly journals that have an unbiased committee of experts to review the articles? If you know nothing about the author, be cautious about using the source.

## EVALUATING A SAMPLE ONLINE SOURCE

Analyze the article, titled "Year-Round Schooling," from an Internet Web site on the topic of education. Here are some questions relevant to the information presented in this article. These questions should help you recognize that many articles from the Internet are not appropriate sources for a research paper.

- Who is the author? Notice that no name is given and no organization is mentioned. Is the author a professional educator, someone who has years of solid experience in the field of education? Could the author be a frustrated parent or an agitated taxpayer?
- When was the article written? Note that the author mentions that students will be "forced to go year-round in January." Is this January of 1998 or 1999?
- Are the "facts" valid? Notice that the article states that "Douglas County is the fastest growing county in the United States." Is this true? How was this determined? Check the accuracy of the following statement which appears in the first paragraph: "New schools cost property owners money, so to reduce this cost the district builds schools that will hold 25 percent more capacity than it can hold at one time." What does this mean?
- Where is Douglas County? Note that the state is not given, so the reader has no frame of reference for understanding the problems that Douglas County is experiencing.
- The article mentions Coyote Creek School? Is this an elementary school, a middle school, or a high school?

Remember that some sites have a social or political agenda, and therefore their documents all have a similar bias. For example, students have discovered that they need to read carefully when they find publications from the American Tobacco Institute or the National Rifle Association.

Scholars warn student researchers to question the validity of articles found on the Internet. According to these experts, cyberspace is full of misinformation. Articles that look authentic, may present outrageous theories, and student researchers may be-

---

**University of Minnesota
Center for Advanced Research
on Language Acquisition**

*Institute of International Studies and Programs*

**What is culture?**

For the purposes of the Intercultural Studies Project, *culture* is defined as the shared patterns of behaviors and interactions, cognitive constructs, and affective understanding that are learned through a process of socialization. These shared patterns identify the members of a group while also distinguishing those of another group.

<http://carla.acad.umn.edu/culture.html>

lieve what they read. The technology has become too advanced to police, so the best advice is to read carefully with a critical eye when searching for online sources.

Student researchers have discovered that sites in the education (.edu) and government (.gov) domains provide reputable documents which work well as sources for college research papers. University faculty and administrators have created valuable Web pages filled with accurate, current information. In the same respect, government agencies provide electronic information on a wide range of topics. The previous sample shows a credible scholarly source from the University of Minnesota.

## AUTHORSHIP OF ONLINE SOURCES

The next step is to carefully evaluate the authorship of a document. In some cases, a site will list the professional organizations that support the author's work, making it possible for you to determine a source's validity. Some documents list the author's professional credentials. Do some research on the author, noting if work by this author appears in the bibliographies of other credible sources. If you search for the author's name on the Web, you may discover that the author's homepage which presents an e-mail address is available. Another approach to determining the author's credibility is to consult one of the bibliographical references such as *Encyclopedia Britannica* that provide a list of authors' names.

Some organizations, such as Magellan and the Argus Clearinghouse, rate various Web sites according to the ease of exploration, coverage, and appeal. These ratings, however, do not cover the reliability or authority of the source. As a researcher, you will have to investigate the legitimacy of your source. Ask your instructor or a reference librarian for help, and search the Web itself for documents that evaluate online sources.

Once you establish that the documents you have chosen are from recognized online sources, the evaluation of your sources becomes easier. When you evaluate your online sources, follow the guidelines for reviewing the accuracy of print sources as presented in this chapter.

## LIMITATIONS OF ONLINE RESEARCH

In addition to being cautious about the validity of an electronic source, you must be aware of the limitations of online research. That is, the World Wide Web only provides a small amount of the available information. Many student researchers believe that all possible information on a topic is available online, but this is not true. Although the Internet—and its subset, the World Wide Web—contain valuable information on an extensive range of topics, the Internet does not contain all of the available information on a topic. Preparing materials for online access requires digitizing, an expensive and time-consuming process. Publishers must limit the availability of their copyrighted materials to protect their financial interests.

INSTRUCTOR'S VIEW

Here's a word of caution about online sources. I have worked with many professors who have studied Internet sources, and they agree that some Web sites should not be used for academic research. The reason is simple. The information on some sites comes from unidentified sources, people who become "instant authors" because they publish on the Internet. This means that anyone, regardless of their background, could pretend to be an expert on a given topic. This puts questionable "facts" into the hands of student researchers who believe that the information they get from Web sites is accurate just because it "came from the computer." In the same respect, though, some Web sites provide accurate information because they are credible sources such as government agencies or universities. It's the student's responsibility to know the source and to question everything they find on the Internet. This is the same strategy that should be used when selecting print sources.

At the present time, less than 5 percent of the scholarly journals and an even smaller percentage of commercial materials are available electronically. This means that for most topics, the Web provides only a starting point for college research. The best advice is to consult the Web, but do not limit your research to this source.

## CONDUCTING FIELD RESEARCH

For many topics it is possible to do *field research*, a type of data collecting conducted on your own, instead of using information collected by others. Information collected during your field research can be used in your paper to support your main points. If you conduct field research, you are demonstrating your interest in the topic as well as your credibility as a researcher and writer. When you use field research in a paper, your reader will notice that you have become involved with the topic, adding to your reliability as an author. Of course, remember to document the information from your field work if you use it in your paper. Specific information on documenting field research appears in Chapter 7 of this manual in the section titled "Works Cited Entries for Nonprint Sources." The most commonly used types of field research for a college paper are observation, surveys, and interviews.

### Observation

Observation is a very useful means of obtaining information for a college paper. When conducting observations, be certain that your methods do not have an impact on what you record. For example, if you are observing the attitudes of commuters on a crowded subway train, do not cause disturbances that will bias what you observe.

Select an appropriate location for your observations. For a paper on the need to restrict teenage drivers, observe the driving habits of high school students as they enter and exit the school parking lot. Use this same site for several days. In your paper, identify where and when the observations took place.

## Surveys

Surveys provide useful information that can serve as evidence to support a point you are trying to make in your paper. It's possible that information from a survey can be used several times within your paper, so try to prepare your questions carefully. To construct an effective survey questionnaire, do the following:

**1.** Determine what you want to know. Thinking through your objectives is critical to constructing a good survey. If you can't identify the information you are seeking, your survey will produce answers that will not be useful in your paper. Remember that the findings from your survey should be used as evidence to support the main points of your paper.

**2.** Write a series of short questions that are directed to the issues of concern. Be certain that your questions are well worded and easy to understand. Ask your instructor to critique your questions before you conduct a sample.

Eliminate bias in your questions by using neutral wording. Avoid language which allows the respondents to detect your position on the topic. Note the following example:

> **Biased Question:** Are you in favor of improving the safety of America's streets by supporting a ban on handguns?   Yes   No
>
> **Neutral Question:** Indicate your response to this question: The sale of handguns must be regulated.
> __strongly agree        __agree        __neutral        __disagree        __strongly disagree

**3.** Field-test your questions before you actually administer your survey. Have a sample of five or six people respond and ask them if your questions were clearly presented.

**4.** Revise your questions and arrange for a second sample group to respond.

**5.** Administer the survey in a neutral environment. Select a representative sample of respondents. The population you survey should vary according to factors such as age, education, occupation, socioeconomic status, and religious or ethnic background. For a survey conducted for a college paper, a population of approximately fifty respondents is adequate.

**6.** Administer your survey and ask the respondents to offer any additional information on the topic. As you review the responses, you may discover that you have to eliminate a few questionnaires. This may happen if the respondent didn't understand the questions or if the respondent didn't respond in a serious manner.

When conducting a survey, try to construct questions that produce concise, quantified answers. For example, you want to write that 78 percent of the thirty-eight citizens who responded to your survey are supporters of welfare reform. Statistics from surveys, even from the informal surveying you conducted, have a powerful impact on readers. Be certain to conduct your survey in an accurate, unbiased manner because this will allow you to produce useful data for your paper. Remember that the survey should not reflect your own views. Use neutral wording and unbiased nonverbal responses when conducting your survey.

For a paper on the role of labor unions, conduct a survey of twenty-five or thirty union members and twenty-five or thirty nonunion members. You may want to ask some background questions (such as how long they have been union members or how much they pay in union dues) before you get to the main questions in your survey. The information you collect can be used to support the points about union membership presented in your paper.

## Interviews

Another widely used method of gaining information is the interview. Your credibility as a researcher is enhanced if you take the time to talk to an authority on your topic, showing the reader that you are willing to go beyond the traditional sources in your search for information. Arranging and conducting an interview requires time and effort, yet it can produce valuable material for your paper.

Although the best interviews occur when you are sitting face to face with the interviewee, it is possible to gather information from a telephone interview. Regardless as to how your information is gathered, it is important to use the information in a conscientious manner. Be certain to present accurate quotations and fair interpretations.

During the interview ask about your interviewee's credentials. Record the information accurately and ask for help with spelling unfamiliar names or terminology. Information about your subject's background will be used in your paper when you present the facts from the interview as shown in the following example:

> China's move to a market-oriented economy will not be easy. In a recent interview Professor Li Chang, an expert in Asian economic policies at Oakland University, stated that China must close unprofitable government industries while encouraging private ownership, foreign trade and investment. He explained that the government will have to resolve the problems of labor unrest and social welfare associated with a failing economy.

When listing an interview in your Works Cited, identify it as a telephone interview or as a personal interview. (See page 89 for a sample.) Follow these guidelines for conducting effective interviews:

**1.** Determine what you want to know. Are you looking for a microbiologist who can explain how bacteria lives in water? Are you looking for several people who will share their impressions of American life during World War II? Are you looking for a psychologist's view on the emotional impact of child abuse?

**2.** Locate an expert to interview. In general, finding an expert on a college campus is not a complicated matter. Ask your instructor or a reference librarian for suggestions. Use the telephone book to find names of local experts.

**3.** When you ask someone for an interview, be certain to identify your topic and your objectives. If people know what you are looking for, they will be able to tell you if they can provide useful information. This helps you avoid the "dead end" interview.

**4.** Prior to the interview, think about the questions you want to ask. Consider what type of information you need for your paper. Prepare a list of specific questions, remembering that the purpose of the interview is to get information to support the main points of your paper. During the interview you may have to improvise on some of the questions.

**5.** Be sure that you are well-prepared for the interview. This may include doing some background reading so you understand the topic and know what approach to take. Bring a tape recorder to record the interviewee's responses, but ask for permission before recording.

**6.** Dress appropriately and conduct yourself in a friendly, polite manner. Show your interest by responding to the interviewee's information, but do not express your own opinions unless you are asked.

**7.** During the interview, listen carefully and take notes. Ask the interviewee to repeat or explain any information that seems unclear.

**8.** Follow up the interview by sending a thank you note, acknowledging your appreciation for the interviewee's time.

## CONSTRUCTING A WORKING BIBLIOGRAPHY

While you are in the process of determining if a source will be appropriate for your paper, you will need to develop a working bibliography. This is a list of sources that you are reviewing for your paper. This list contains the titles and all of the publication information for sources which you may or may not use in your paper. If your list seems limited, do more research or expand your topic because it may be too narrow. If your list seems too expansive, you will need to limit your topic by eliminating subtopics that cause the information to move away from the main point.

INSTRUCTOR'S VIEW

Some students don't recognize the importance of doing a general review of all available sources before deciding which ones to use in a paper. They try to skip the preliminary step of constructing a working bibliography because they don't want to invest the time and effort it takes to do a really thorough review before they begin writing. All they want to do is to find a minimum number of sources to toss into the paper so they can get the paper written.

Remember to keep your source information organized. Some students prefer to list their bibliographic data on note cards because this provides an easy way to sort and organize information, while others use a research journal or logbook for recording information. Determine a method of organization early in the research writing process and stay with it. Be certain to save the computer printouts containing bibliographic information because you may need these details when you list your sources.

As you begin to read and evaluate your sources, you will start eliminating some from your working bibliography. Others will be eliminated as you write the paper because you will discover that all of the sources are not appropriate for your topic. As a general guideline, remember that a working bibliography should list two or three times as many sources as you will actually use in the paper.

A working bibliography helps you avoid the last minute surprises that often accompany library research. By compiling a list of your sources early in the research process, you will know which ones are available and you will be able to develop a general idea of how well each source will work into your paper.

At this stage of the research process, it's a good idea to assess your knowledge of the topic. Ask yourself three basic questions:

What do I know about the topic?
What questions do I have about the topic?
What information do I need to better understand the topic?

## Some Reminders

- Ask questions so you will understand the requirements of your research writing assignment. Follow your instructor's recommendations for selecting a topic.
- Allow plenty of time to think and plan when focusing your topic and selecting your sources. Talk to the reference librarian about your topic and evaluate your sources before using them in your paper.
- Remember that many online sources provide a wealth of information, yet many others are of questionable value. Use well-documented online materials from reputable sources. Your job as a research writer is to make decisions about the credibility of your sources.
- Keep your source material organized in the early stages of the research process. This will help you avoid wasting time as you review your material and work with your sources.

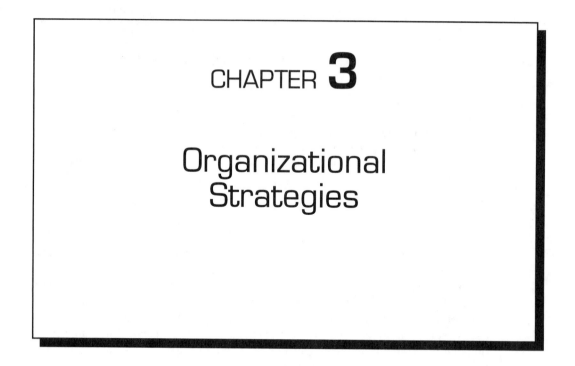

# CHAPTER **3**

# Organizational Strategies

## REVIEWING YOUR SOURCES

Now that you have constructed a working bibliography, you should have some general ideas about your topic. As you continue to work with your sources, your ideas will develop and soon you will be able to prepare a preliminary plan or outline. You should start thinking about possible ideas for a thesis statement, the single focus that will unify your paper.

Your next task is to review each source to determine if it presents information relevant to the points you wish to present in your paper. Below are some steps to follow when reading your source material.

### Previewing the Material

Quickly skim through each article and identify the author's main points. Remember that skimming is rapid reading designed to provide a basic overview of the material. When previewing your source material, look for the following:

- Information about the author
- Names of experts in the field and names of other authors
- Titles of related articles
- Key words related to the topic
- Subheadings and categories within the topic

- Related issues and topics
- Bibliographic information which leads to other sources
- Strategies for focusing or narrowing the topic
- Ideas for a thesis statement
- Reasons which support a thesis statement

As you preview your sources, make a mark in the margin or attach a note if you find significant points that may be useful in your paper. If previewing reveals that the article doesn't present information that follows the focus you are trying to present in your paper, don't use the article. (Do not discard the article, however, because you may need to refer to it later.)

Some students make the mistake of using information that is only partially related to the main point of the paper. You may be tempted to do this because you don't want to go back to the library to locate better sources or you don't want to waste the money you spent making copies of the articles. You should recognize, however, that using information that does not follow the focus of the paper creates disorganization and incoherence. The readers of your paper will detect that the content doesn't fit, so eliminate unrelated information during the previewing stage.

### Reading Sources Carefully

Once you have previewed your sources and selected the best ones, it's time to read each source carefully to determine the author's main points. In addition, read the final paragraphs carefully because they may present an important summary of the material.

Make certain that you understand the material. Avoid misinterpreting what the author has written by reading carefully and by thinking about the information. Use the strategies for active reading presented in this chapter. If you find sections of the article confusing, go back and read them again. Remember that you must understand the source material before you can use it intelligently in your paper.

Students often stop reading a source after the first few paragraphs because they think that they have the basic idea, believing that they can just pull sections from an article to use in a paper. This practice creates a rambling, unfocused paper that may present a faulty interpretation of the source material. To avoid these problems, read each source completely and carefully. Be careful about making photocopies of sources you find in the early stages of the research process. Students often rush to make copies, often wasting time and money on materials that are not useful.

### Active Reading Strategies

In order to read sources carefully, you must employ active reading strategies. Question and analyze the material. Some ways in which you can analyze source material follow.

**Determine the author's purpose:** Is the author trying to inform? Entertain? Persuade?

**Identify the main idea:** What is the author's position?

**Review the author's strategies:** How does the author develop the ideas? Does the author use examples? Expert opinion? Statistics?

**Underline or highlight significant points:** Are you thinking about the information before marking it in an attempt to better understand the selection? What are the most important points?

**Respond to the ideas:** What is your view of the selection? Were you exposed to new ideas? Were any ideas confusing or unclear? (Record your responses in your research journal or on your note cards. Make notes in the margins of the selection.)

**Read the selection again:** Can you discover something new by rereading the selection? What points stand out?

## USING A RESEARCH JOURNAL

You may want to use a research journal to record your thoughts as you prepare your paper. This journal should be a simple notebook which serves as a log of information

---

### READ—THINK—WRITE

Title of Source _____     Author _____

Topic _____

What is the author's main point? _____

_____

List notes for the following:

| What does the author say? | What do you think? |
| --- | --- |
| _____ | _____ |
| _____ | _____ |
| _____ | _____ |
| _____ | _____ |
| _____ | _____ |

and ideas. Some students prefer to store a research journal on a disk. Regardless of the format, the journal is a place to store information related to your paper. Many students have found that a research journal encourages them to think through ideas related to the topic while giving a sense of organization and focus.

The writing in the journal is for you—not for a reader—so you should feel free to explore, question, complain, or critique. As you start your research, the journal will encourage you to present your thoughts on the information you are finding. These ideas can become a valuable part of your paper, content that makes your work unique because it presents your personal interpretations and inferences on the topic. In fact, many students take sections of information from their research journals and use them in drafts of their papers.

The following prewriting exercise is designed to help you process the information from your research. Complete one of these forms for each source, and then use the information in your paper.

## NOTETAKING

Notetaking practices vary from one student to the next. Some students have developed a system of storing their notes on a computer disk, a practice that allows easy access to the information when drafting a paper. Other students make copies of relevant articles and write their notes in the margins of the articles. This approach is adequate, but it's not as effective as the use of note cards because it doesn't allow for information to be sorted and organized. By contrast, note cards can be sorted easily, allowing you to discard those which present irrelevant or repeated information. Furthermore, note cards enable you to arrange and rearrange the order of your material, which greatly improves the organization of your paper.

Even though the practice of using note cards may seem outdated in the age of electronic data, students who are well organized rely on note cards to keep track of their information. These students prepare cards with bold headings and carefully labeled subheadings to organize the material they are going to use when writing their papers, recognizing that this approach provides a good beginning for a successful paper. The best approach is to limit each card to one main idea because this makes it easier to sort the cards into groups of similar ideas.

The important point about notetaking, however, is to establish a system for jotting down information and for keeping it organized. The notes should be brief and should be keyed to a source so you can refer back to that source if you have questions about the content.

Your note cards or your notes should contain bibliographic information so you can identify the source. Be certain that this information is accurately recorded so you will not encounter problems when preparing the reference list for your paper.

Problems with plagiarism and academic dishonesty often start in the research stage of the writing process when students copy information from sources and fail to distinguish between their own wording and that of the source. To avoid this difficulty, put quotation marks around the wording that comes from a source. Remember that you must use quotation marks for three or more consecutive words copied from a source. (For additional information, refer to the section titled "Using Direct Quotations" in Chapter 5.)

## SAMPLE NOTE CARDS

---

**AFFIRMATIVE ACTION**

*Denies Rights of Employers*

*Bovard, James  "Here Comes the Goon Squad."*
*American Spectator July '96 page 36+*

*Critics believe must be free from govt. reg. mandating hiring; Office of Federal Contract Compliance is a "monster which victimizes American companies" (example: Commonwealth Aluminum, Carolina Steel)*

---

**AFFIRMATIVE ACTION**

*Counterargument/Advance Minorities*

*Amselle, Jorge  "A Quota By Any Other Name." National Review*
*Feb 26 '96 page 20+*

*Supporters argue that AA policies necessary to promote minorities; economic and social benefit because victimized by society*

---

**AFFIRMATIVE ACTION**

*Court Decisions against Affirmative Action*

*Lederman, Douglas  "Growing Attacks on Affirmative Action"*
*Chronicle of Higher Education April 26, '96 page A27*

*"U.S. Court of Appeals for the Fifth Circuit ruled that the University of Texas law school can no longer use racial preferences as a basis for its admissions policies"; result is the university will suffer financial penalties if financial aid or admissions is based on race*

---

INSTRUCTOR'S VIEW

I always tell my students that the organizational strategies that require extra time in the early stages of the research writing process will help them avoid confusion as the paper progresses. The end result, of course, is that they can produce better papers if they work on the preliminary steps of conducting appropriate research and organizing their material. I emphasize that the student's ability to work with reference sources is important not only in the college coursework but also in the workplace.

## THINKING ABOUT THE MATERIAL

Before you begin writing, take time to think about the information you have read. Discuss the information with someone else because this allows you to discover what you know and what you don't know about the topic. A useful approach is to explain information related to your topic to another student, focusing on the main points you want to develop in your paper. Many instructors arrange for students to work in groups because they want students to talk and think about the material before they begin writing a paper. It's difficult to produce a good paper if you don't understand the topic, so learn as much as possible about your topic before you begin writing.

## PREWRITING EXERCISE TO FOCUS A TOPIC

After reading and taking notes, analyze what you know about your topic before you begin writing. Many students find that preparing a preliminary list of ideas is helpful in determining the focus of the paper. This can be done through a prewriting exercise, which requires about fifteen minutes of freewriting.

The following is an example of freewriting that was prepared before a paper on affirmative action was written. (The paper, titled "The Threat of Affirmative Action," is a sample student paper in this book.)

Through this prewriting exercise, the student writer explored the various aspects of affirmative action and arrived at a preliminary thesis statement. These notes indicate that the student focused the topic on the area of affirmative action and employment, discovering that the topic should not discuss discrimination in housing or unfair lending practices by mortgage companies. As you can see, prewriting is a good way to narrow a topic and to explore ideas for a thesis statement.

AFFIRMATIVE ACTION

Although discrimination outlawed by Civil Rights laws, do minorities really have equal opportunities? Throughout the years minorities were denied rights

- —housing so they don't have to live in high crime, poor areas
    - —Do minorities face discrimination in housing?
    - —Are minorities subject to unfair lending practices from mortgage companies?
- —employment opportunities
- —well paying jobs
- —education (need for good schools and college scholarships)
    - —serious need for equal educational standards
    - —minorities can't succeed without education

Affirmative Action plan provides equal opportunities and minorities begin to prosper. Are Affirmative Action programs unfair to nonminorities? Do they suffer from reverse discrimination because minorities are given preferences?
Employers believe programs give advantages to minorities who often are not qualified for the job.

Does Affirmative Action have a negative impact?

1. enforced government quotas divide society and create tension
2. creates difficulties for business owners who must hire according to govt. quotas, not always best qualified applicant
3. harmful to minorities (damages self respect)
4. unfair to nonminorities who are better qualified

Does Affirmative Action have a positive impact?

1. Companies want diversified, multiracial pool of employees
2. Ends unequal treatment in the workplace

Legal attacks on Affirmative Action result in changes in law

- —nonminority company fights for contracts given to minority company

## WRITING WITH A THESIS

A library research paper requires you to conduct a thorough review of the literature on your topic and to present information which supports a major premise or a thesis. Whether you are preparing an academic paper or a workplace report, remember that research writing requires you to present an analysis and an interpretation of the information you have researched. This means that the paper must be more than a general summary of source information: It must take a position on the topic and present evidence to support that view. In this way, your work becomes an "argument paper."

As a research writer, your job is to persuade the reader to accept your position on the topic. Take the time to review the following elements of argument writing and try to incorporate these ideas into your work:

1. **Thesis:** Present an effective thesis and maintain that focus throughout the paper.
2. **Support:** Use convincing evidence to support the thesis.
3. **Author's credibility:** Show yourself to be a believable writer by using a style which "talks" to your reader.
4. **Audience:** Develop an awareness of your reader's response. Anticipate the readers' questions and have the answers ready.

## Presenting an Effective Thesis and Controlling Idea

As you know, the thesis of your paper is the *controlling idea*, the premise that gives a focus to your paper and determines what source material you will present. Generally expressed in one sentence, the *thesis* states your position on the topic and serves as an organizational tool. It predicts the general development of the paper, giving direction to you as the writer as well as serving as a guide for your readers.

During the early stages of your research writing, your thesis may be a preliminary statement that gives a focus to your work. As you review your sources and explore various subtopics, you may need to modify your thesis.

Without an effective thesis, a research paper lacks a clear direction. You can lose control of your topic when your thesis is not limited and focused, resulting in a paper that presents massive amounts of research material but lacks a unifying idea. In most cases, an unlimited thesis is too broad for a college research paper. This may cause you, as the author, to become confused about the topic and to include irrelevant information which, in turn, confuses the reader.

By contrast, an effective thesis enables you to work with your content in a focused, organized manner. It allows you to develop your position fully and to avoid drifting away from the major premise of the paper. An effective thesis forecasts the paper's organizational structure, giving the reader information about what to expect in the paper.

Review this example to get a better understanding of how the thesis functions. If you are working with the topic of child abuse, for example, your thesis can move your paper in a number of directions. Consider the following possibilities:

A. Child abuse is a critical social issue.
B. Child abuse must be stopped.
C. Child abuse causes serious long-term problems.
D. Child abuse occurs in all realms of society.
E. Child abuse is difficult to stop.

Which statement presents the best thesis?

As you can see, each statement presents a different way to approach the same topic, but the strongest statement for a college research paper is statement E: Child abuse is difficult to stop.

Statements A and B are too obvious. No one would argue against these points because everyone knows that child abuse is a serious problem which must be stopped. Statements C and D would lead to some interesting psychological and sociological discussions about the causes and effects of child abuse. However, these statements do not present a strong premise because they are facts, not opinions. Remember that the thesis must express an opinion.

Statement E presents an effective thesis because it takes a solid position; a reader can argue against it. There is research evidence to support, as well as to refute, this statement.

## Working with a Preliminary Thesis Statement

It may be necessary for you to modify your thesis statement while you are working through the process of researching, writing, and revising. When you first begin your research, the thesis is a tentative statement that provides enough direction to help you get started. As you learn about the topic and find source information, you may discover that your early ideas about the topic won't work. You may need to change the thesis because you find that the focus is too broad or that the evidence you have found won't support the thesis. In some cases, student writers have abandoned the preliminary thesis altogether because they have discovered that the source information doesn't support the thesis.

Once your research is complete, you can finalize your thesis statement before writing the paper. Remember, however, to be flexible with your thesis while you are in the early stages of research. It's better to modify a preliminary thesis than to write a paper which has an ineffective thesis.

## Supporting the Thesis with Reasons

The purpose of a research paper is to present evidence which supports the thesis. This allows you, as a research writer, to present an effective argument to your reader.

As you conduct your research, you are looking for source information that tells *why* the thesis is true. This evidence is used to develop the paragraphs which support the thesis, and it should persuade the reader to accept your position on the topic.

Use *reasons* to support the thesis. Examples may be interesting, but they do not take the place of reasons and explanations in a research paper. When an example is presented without a reason, the information is not effectively conveyed and the reader misses the point. A common error for student writers is to assume that the reader will "read between the lines" to understand what a paragraph means. This breakdown in communication between the reader and the writer results in a poor paper.

When you are looking for reasons, ask yourself this question: Why is the thesis true? If your supporting paragraphs answer this question, they are following the direction of the thesis.

Review these sample thesis statements and supporting reasons. Note that opposing views of victim impact statements are presented. Sample A supports the use of victim impact statements in the courtroom, while Sample B presents the opposite view.

### SAMPLE A

**Thesis:** Victim impact statements should be allowed in the courtroom.

Reason 1. Victim impact statements give the victim and the victim's family the opportunity to express their rage and sense of loss.

Reason 2. Victim impact statements encourage judges to give stiffer penalties as they become more aware of the victim's suffering.

Reason 3. Victim impact statements force the accused to face the effects of the crime.

### SAMPLE B

**Thesis:** Victim impact statements should not be allowed in the courtroom.

Reason 1. Victim impact statements are inappropriate in the courtroom because they are too emotional.

Reason 2. Video taped statements can work against the accused years after being sentenced for the crime.

Reason 3. Victim impact statements neglect the rights of homeless victims and favor the victims whose families are actively seeking justice.

The reasons that support the thesis give direction to your paper and therefore should serve as the topic sentences for your paragraphs. Remember that each reason may be developed in one paragraph or in several paragraphs, depending on the amount of material you must present to make your point. As you develop each paragraph, use specific information from your source.

## Some Reminders

- When selecting sources for your paper, preview each source. Look for information which follows the focus of your thesis.
- Take the time to read your sources carefully. Remember that you can't use source material intelligently unless you understand the information.
- Be alert when you prepare your note cards. Problems with plagiarism and academic dishonesty often begin in the early stages of the research writing process.
- As you sort your note cards, attempt to determine an organizational pattern for your paper. This is the first step in creating an outline.

## PLANNING CHECKLIST

This checklist can help you work through the research writing process in an efficient, organized manner. Note the due dates and jot down notes to remember.

|                             | Due Date | Notes |
| --------------------------- | -------- | ----- |
| Selecting a Topic           |          |       |
| Doing Preliminary Reading   |          |       |
| Limiting the Topic          |          |       |
| Formulating a Thesis        |          |       |
| Locating Sources            |          |       |
| Evaluating Sources          |          |       |
| Preparing an Outline        |          |       |
| Drafting                    |          |       |
| Revising and Editing        |          |       |
| Proofreading                |          |       |
| Preparing a Final Copy      |          |       |

# CHAPTER 4

# Writing
# Strategies

## DEVELOPING SUPPORTING PARAGRAPHS

As you know, you must support your thesis with reasons that relate directly to the main point you are trying to present. Once you have determined the supporting points, the next step is to develop your ideas by writing a paragraph or several paragraphs for each idea.

Your paragraphs will present the information you have found in your sources. In order to present an effective argument, your paragraphs should include examples, statistics, and authority opinions. In addition, presenting the opposing view through a counterargument is a good strategy to follow when preparing an argument paper.

### Using Examples As Evidence

Examples serve as solid evidence to support a point you are trying to make in your paper. The examples may be taken from source material, from interviews with knowledgeable people, or from your personal experiences. Most student writers are familiar with using examples when writing research papers. The weakness, however, is that many writers fail to adequately explain their examples, allowing the information to stand alone without the benefit of an appropriate introduction or conclusion.

When developing a paragraph through the use of an example, remember to keep the example brief. Two or three sentences should be sufficient for most examples. Another point to remember is to avoid using too many examples. Instructors readily recognize when you are trying to "pad" your paper by filling paragraph after paragraph with lengthy examples. The overuse of examples is a signal that you are trying to avoid the more difficult content that requires explanation and analysis.

The most effective method for using an example is to present it after you have stated a main point. In most cases, the main point serves as the topic sentence of your paragraph by introducing the reader to the idea you wish to develop. The example serves as an illustration of that point. Of course, your example should be followed by an explanation which relates to the thesis statement. This provides a focus for your information and it ties together the example and the thesis, helping your reader understand why you presented the example.

Consider how examples are used in these sample paragraphs:

### SAMPLE A: POLICE BRUTALITY

The problem of police brutality in American cities can be reduced through extensive reform. This requires police departments to change the practices of the past and to adopt new approaches to law enforcement. The cities of Philadelphia and Houston, for example, have been successful in reducing racially related police brutality cases through a program which puts a large number of black officers on the force. This approach includes educating law enforcement officers about social as well as criminal problems (Gest 49). The success of these cities reveals that it is possible to reduce police brutality.

### SAMPLE B: POVERTY IN THE UNITED STATES

The issue of poverty in the United States must be examined more carefully because thousands of full-time workers who exist on a reduced standard of living are not counted in the government's poverty figures. According to a 1997 report commissioned by the Department of Agriculture, the government's misleading poverty figures actually "disguise the problem of the working poor" because the figures fall far below the official level (Schwartz and Rider 21). This means that the government's numbers do not present an accurate picture of poverty in this country. To illustrate this point, consider the situation of Mary and Fred Sparks, a married couple with two young children, who live in San Diego on a combined annual income of $21,400. He works in a warehouse and she is employed by a fast food restaurant. This family rents a meager two bedroom apartment, and often does not have enough money for food, gas, or clothing. Their medical and dental care is postponed indefinitely ("American Poverty" 138–41). Since the Sparks' income is above the official poverty line for a family of four, they are not classified as being "poor" by the federal government's standards. As a result, they do not qualify for assistance programs for child care, health care, or housing. The government must revise its definition of poverty so that people like the Sparks family can enjoy a better standard of living.

These sample paragraphs indicate how an example should be used. Note that a topic sentence and other explanatory material are presented *before* the example. Concluding sentences present an interpretation of the example and some commentary. An exception to this guideline is when an example is used in the introductory paragraph. An important point to remember is that an example cannot stand alone: it must have an introduction and a concluding comment. This gives you the opportunity to present your interpretation of the example.

Many writers use wording such as "for example" or "to illustrate this point" when presenting an example. This wording helps the reader follow the direction of the paragraph and serves as an effective transitional device.

### Using Expert Opinion As Evidence

An important type of evidence is *authoritative testimony*, the use of expert opinion to support the thesis. When using this type of evidence, select authorities on your topic and briefly present their credentials. Remember that the person must be an expert on the topic, not in a related area. If you find authorities who present conflicting information, do more research so you can present one expert while refuting the other. As the researcher, your job is to analyze the material and to make informed judgments about its value. Review the wording used in these examples of authoritative support:

> David Neumark, a University of Michigan economist who has studied global unemployment, notes that job-tenure rates throughout the world have not declined significantly within the past two years (21).

> Harlem should be restored as the center of black culture for residents, businesses, and tourists, according to Deborah Wright, president and chief executive officer of the Upper Manhattan Empowerment Zone Development Corp. ("New York" 8).

### Authority Opinion and Direct Quotation

Another method of using authoritative support is through direct quotation. Using the exact words of an expert adds credibility to your paper, but you must remember to quote the source accurately. This sample is based on an article by Kessler titled "FDA's Progress Sets New Standard."

> Dr. David Kessler, former Food and Drug Administration Chief, described the changes he instituted in getting FDA approval for drugs. He states that his agency had achieved "world-record time for drug approvals by making the pharmaceutical industry support the enactment of drug-maker fees which are used to pay for additional FDA drug reviewers" ("FDA's Progress" 9).

If your expert was quoted in another source, the citation must indicate this. When using a quotation from another source, you must acknowledge who said the words and note the source in which the quotation first appeared in your Works Cited. See "Secondary Sources" on pages 24–25 and 71–72 of this manual.

The following sample demonstrates how to present authority opinion that was stated as a direct quotation in the original source. This sample is based on an article by Larry Bivins. Bivins interviewed Rev. Clayton Butts and used Butts' exact words in his article.

New York City was one of the last of the six empowerment zones to begin the renewal project. Some residents believe that the city's bureaucracy caused the delay. According to Rev. Clayton Butts, pastor of the Abyssinian Baptist Church in Harlem, "If it has to do with picking up a piece of paper, it'll lay on the ground for six weeks if politics are involved" (qtd. in Bivins: 8A). These words reveal the frustration city residents experience.

## USING COUNTERARGUMENT AND CONTRADICTORY EVIDENCE

A well-constructed research paper presents both supportive as well as contradictory evidence. This strategy is important because it builds your credibility as a writer when you show the reader that you are aware of the other side of your argument. The reader sees you as a fair-minded writer who has researched the topic completely, as someone who is not trying to suppress evidence that opposes the thesis. When contradictory evidence is used effectively, it strengthens your position.

When using contradictory evidence or a counterargument, remember that this information changes the direction of your paper. That is, you must be careful to signal the reader through the use of transitional wording that you are taking a different position. Remember to return to your thesis statement after you have presented the counterargument, as shown in the following example:

### THESIS: CASINO GAMBLING SHOULD REMAIN LEGAL

Although casino gambling has much support because of its economic benefits, some citizens believe that legalized gambling must be stopped. Opponents of casino gambling feel that this activity causes serious problems for the gambler and for the family. According to Valerie Lorenz, Executive Director of the Compulsive Gambling Center in Baltimore, "Innocent recreation and fun becomes addiction which leads to financial ruin, lying, stealing, and constant emotional pain and stress" (6). Supporters of casino gambling recognize that there is some truth to Ms. Lorenz's concerns because they know that legalization brings greater accessibility. They concede that some gamblers go beyond their limits and cause financial and emotional problems for their families, yet they emphasize that the problem is with a pathological personality, not with the institution of gambling. Most mental health professionals generally agree that a psychological addiction to another behavior would develop if casino gambling were unavailable. Dr. Richard J. Rosenthal, author of *Gambling Behavior and Problem Gambling* and doctor of psychiatry at the UCLA School of Medicine, states that we should not blame legalized gambling. He notes that we should view compulsive gamblers as a "reflection of the deeper changes which are taking place in society" (221). This means that a compulsive person will get into trouble, whether it be with alcohol, drugs, gambling, or some other vice. Other supporters of casinos argue that there is a vast difference between social and compulsive gambling. The issue is, why deny the total population a relaxing, enjoyable pastime when just a small segment has problems controlling their wagering? Casino gambling must remain legal because it offers appropriate entertainment for American adults.

### Using Statistics As Evidence

Statistics are an important element of argument because most numbers present a clear, objective picture and serve as solid evidence to support the thesis. Here are some guidelines to follow when using statistics in your paper:

- Present numbers which are relevant to the point you are trying to make.
- Avoid confusing or irrelevant numbers.
- Begin with an introduction so the reader knows why you are presenting the statistics.
- Present comments which explain the statistics and offer an interpretation.
- Identify the source and the date of the information in the text of your paper. This information helps the reader understand the source of your data.
- Use statistics sparingly. Too many numbers may confuse the reader and detract from your argument.
- Use current statistics (within the past five or six years if possible) unless you are presenting an historical perspective.

#### SAMPLE A: TEEN DRIVING

Studies of teen driving indicate that serious problems need attention. A 1997 report by the Center for Disease Prevention and Control investigated the rate at which sixteen- to twenty-year-old drivers are involved in traffic fatalities. Although young people comprised only 6.7 percent of the total number of drivers, they were involved in 14 percent of the fatal accidents ("Death Toll" 7A). According to this information, young drivers have a disproportionately high number of fatal accidents. These numbers support the position that states should adopt stricter licensing regulations.

#### SAMPLE B: WELFARE REFORM

A battle exists between welfare reform and defense spending. According to the Center on Budget and Policy Priorities, the allocation for 1996 through 2002 indicates that the spending for low-income programs makes up 23 percent of the nondefense budget, but will receive 53 percent of all budget cuts (Levin). This means that programs for poor Americans are being cut at a higher rate than any other budget category.

## PREPARING AN OUTLINE

Should you create an outline first or should you explore your topic through prewriting before establishing an outline? Some students create an outline after they have done some preliminary writing. This can be a useful approach because it allows you to explore your topic and to discover what you need to explain to your readers. Both approaches are valid, so use the method that is best suited for your style. (Refer to the prewriting exercises in Chapter 3.)

Once you have developed a thesis statement, it's time to organize your information into an outline. Similar to notetaking, outlining is another essential step in the research writing process that allows for individual strategies. Most students find that the type of outline or plan they use depends on their instructors' requirements or on strategies used for previous papers.

There are many types of outlines, ranging from the formal outline to the informal list of ideas. In addition, there are many ways to organize information for a paper. The important point, however, is for you to establish a plan early in the writing process because this will give you a blueprint to follow even though it may be informal and flexible. Of course, you will probably need to modify your plan as you move through the writing process, but an outline in the early stages of writing will help you identify the direction of your paper.

Through outlining you are attempting to divide a complex topic into smaller, logical sections. If you have well-prepared note cards, you can use the main points from the cards' headings and subheadings to develop the structure of your outline. You will not be able to construct a useful outline until you have identified how your topic will be divided, so take the time to analyze your information. Remember that it's much easier to write and rewrite an outline than it is to write and rewrite a disorganized paper.

Review the following sample outline taken from the student paper on affirmative action. Notice that both the formal topic outline and the informal list of ideas begins with the thesis statement. That is, the thesis should serve as the foundation of the outline.

Outlines must present a logical division of ideas. This means that you must present at least two points when you divide a subtopic. If you have a point A, you must have a point B. If you have a point 1, you must have a point 2. Review the following sample formal outline and compare it to the informal list of ideas that follows it:

**FORMAL OUTLINE**

THESIS: Affirmative action policies have a negative impact on society

INTRODUCTION: Background information on civil rights laws and explanation of affirmative action policies

- I. Reasons to support thesis
  - A. Unfair to nonminorities
    1. More qualified candidates are excluded
    2. Forces employers to discriminate
    3. Example of New Jersey teacher who lost job
  - B. Negative impact on employer's rights
    1. Government regulations mandate who is hired
    2. Workplace suffers
       a. Minorities used to fill quota
       b. Going against good business sense
    3. Programs victimize large corporations
       a. Regulation of business is nonproductive
       b. Taxpayers resent the wasting of money

    C. Quotas harmful to minorities
       1. Qualified minorities treated as tokens
       2. Damaging to self-respect
    D. Tension within society due to affirmative action programs
       1. Result in divided society
       2. Problems in workplace
       3. Laws don't promote racial harmony
II. Arguments against thesis and refutations
    A. Affirmative action supporters claim programs essential
       1. Concession: Minorities not given equal opportunities
       2. Refutation: Reverse discrimination is not answer
    B. Discrimination limits minorities' job opportunities
       1. Concession: Inequality part of past; minorities did suffer
       2. Refutation: Companies now want diversification
       3. Refutation: Government should not decide
III. Additional reasons to support thesis
    A. Personal experience
       1. Tool and die worker not qualified for job
       2. Frustration for manager and worker
    B. Political and legal attacks against affirmative action
       1. Example from University of Texas law school
       2. Impact on minorities

## INFORMAL LIST OF IDEAS

TOPIC: Affirmative action
THESIS: Affirmative action policies have a negative impact on society
    —Introduce topic by presenting background information on civil rights law
    —Present reasons why thesis is true
       1. Program is unfair to minorities
       2. Policies have negative impact on employers
       3. Harmful to minorities because treated like tokens
       4. Divides society and creates uneasiness

---

### STUDENT'S VIEW

For years I heard teachers tell me about the importance of outlining, but it always just seemed like more busy work, a way of dragging out the writing of a research paper. If an outline was required, I would construct one after the paper was written. This wasn't too easy, however, because it was always hard to figure out what I had done in the paper. Everything seemed confused, but the paper was finished so I didn't worry about it until I saw that my grade was low. My approach changed when I started working with an instructor who required an outline before any writing can begin. Now I use an outline as a checklist. I mark off the sections I have completed, so I have a fairly good idea of where I'm trying to go with my paper. Also, the outline helps me avoid two problems I always had in previous papers: I would repeat information and not even know that I covered it earlier, and I would completely forget to include some main points. So, an outline has become useful.

      5. Causes serious political and legal problems
      6. Explain personal experience at tool and die plant
—Discuss counterarguments and refute them
      1. Supporters claim programs are essential
      2. Minorities suffer from discrimination
—Conclude with comments on voters' preferences to stop affirmative action programs

## WRITING A FIRST DRAFT

You are ready to write a first draft once you have reviewed your source material, constructed a tentative plan or outline, and arrived at a preliminary thesis statement. These preparatory steps are essential in getting you ready to produce a draft that is more than a confusing collection of quotations. Review the following strategies for preparing a first draft:

1. View your first draft as your initial effort, as something that will be changed and modified as you work through the writing process.
2. Allow plenty of time by starting early. Do not wait until the last minute.
3. Follow your outline or plan. Keep track of what you have completed and have a clear view of where you are going.
4. Ignore spelling and punctuation in this first draft. Write freely so you can express your ideas without worrying about mechanics.
5. Skip lines and leave wide margins so you can insert material and make changes.
6. Emphasize your thesis statement and remember that the thesis ties the ideas in the paper together. Post your thesis in bold letters to remind you of your direction.
7. Modify the thesis if it doesn't seem to be working. If the content strays from the thesis, think about what you are trying to present. Determine if the content really belongs with the thesis.
8. Try to keep your use of source material organized and accurate. If you are sloppy with your sources in this first draft, the problem is difficult to correct in later drafts.

Remember that this first draft is the foundation of your paper. It's a starting point, not a finished product. As you are preparing your first draft, you will need to be concerned about your use of sources.

### Some Reminders

- Support your thesis with reasons that relate to the main point you are trying to present in each paragraph. To present an effective argument, your paragraphs should include examples, statistics, and authority opinions. Your paper also should include the opposing view.
- Use outlining to help you divide and organize your information. Preparing an outline is worth the time because it's much easier to rewrite an outline than it is to rewrite a disorganized paper.

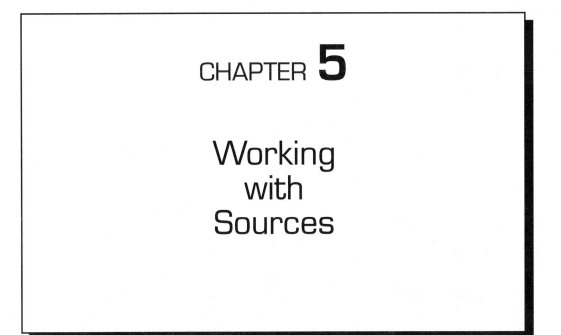

CHAPTER **5**

# Working
# with
# Sources

## LOCATING SOURCE MATERIAL TO SUPPORT THE THESIS

Now that you have focused your topic through preliminary reading, it's time to begin doing some serious research. This means taking the time to work through one source after the next until you find those that provide information to support your thesis. This step requires you to

- Think about your topic
- Ask yourself questions about the topic
- Anticipate concerns your reader will have
- Make several trips to the library
- Review unfamiliar sources
- Reject sources not appropriate for your topic.

This stage of the research process is when some students start to cut corners, believing that they can create a good paper by using the first five sources they find. You should know that poor research is evident in a paper—there's no way to hide it.

Remember to keep your material organized by creating a system for taking notes. Maybe you'll use a legal pad, a spiral notebook, or note cards. The important point, however, is for you to devise a system and use it so you can keep your materials and sources organized. If you are using a research journal, remember to record your responses to your sources. As you know, this will help you avoid confusion and, frustration as you prepare your paper.

## USING SOURCES FOR A RESEARCH PAPER

When instructors assign a paper requiring "outside sources," they want you to go beyond what you already know about the topic. Whether they call it a "term paper" or a "research paper," the product is essentially the same. Instructors expect you to read extensively, analyze the authors' points, and make judgments about the information. The paper you prepare should present *your* views on the topic, supported by facts, statistics, and expert opinion.

As you integrate source material into your paper, identify the source by providing a citation. The citation contains information which allows your reader to locate the complete reference listed at the end of the paper. Before you begin working with citations and reference lists, determine if your instructor prefers a specific style of documentation.

## DOCUMENTATION STYLES

Documentation styles vary according to academic disciplines. Examples in this manual are based on MLA (Modern Language Association) style, which is used for papers in language, literature, and most courses in humanities (philosophy and religion) and the fine arts (music, art, and theater). For other courses, you may be required to use another form of documentation. For example, APA (American Psychological Association) style is used in psychology, business, and in the social sciences. CBE (Council of Biology Editors) style is used for biological sciences. Most papers for history courses use the footnote system. Other disciplines such as the applied sciences (mathematics, physics, engineering, medicine, chemistry, and computer science) use the number system.

### MLA Style

Scholars of language and literature focus on the work; therefore, MLA style uses a *citation* (also known as a *parenthetical reference*) listing the author of the work and the page number. This simple, concise system is adequate for most undergraduate work and is used frequently in composition courses. Once you become familiar with MLA style, making variations for other systems presents few problems. The following example demonstrates the parenthetical reference of MLA style:

> Students should understand theatrical conventions of past eras. As a specialist writes, "Theaters in ancient Greece or Elizabethan England were nothing at all like our modern theaters in physical construction, properties, or lighting and other electronics" (Cooper 74).
>
> Citation        Author  Page

The information in parentheses indicates that the quoted material came from page 74 of a book by Cooper. Notice the style for punctuation: quotation marks appear first, followed by the author's last name and page number in parentheses with no comma separating the two items, and ending with a period. In MLA style, the list of sources that appears at the end of a paper is known as the Works Cited list.

### Author/Date System (APA Style)

Commonly used by business as well as by the physical and social sciences, the Author/Date system follows the specifications advocated in the *Publication Manual of the American Psychological Association*, also known as the APA style manual. Comparable to MLA style noted above, this system uses citations consisting of the author's last name, the year of publication, and the page number.

Timeliness is essential to disciplines using the Author/Date system. The focus, therefore, is on the date rather than on the author as in MLA style. Punctuation for the Author/Date system is shown in the following examples. Note that this system uses an abbreviation for the word page (p.), whereas MLA style presents only the numeral.

> Discussing the issue of risk management in the Information Age, Professor Graham (1997) of the Harvard School of Public Health writes, "A good example of skewed priorities is our treatment of electromagnetic fields" (p. 5B).

> The real difficulty of making ill-informed public health decisions is the "statistical murder of citizens who die or suffer from proven, yet neglected hazards" (Graham, 1997, p. 5B).

Note that when the author's name and date appear in your text, they are omitted from the parenthetical reference, as shown in the Graham quotation above. Use commas to separate the information in the parenthetical reference, as demonstrated in the second example.

According to the Author/Date system, when using two or more works published in a given year by the same author, attach a lower case letter to each: 1997a, 1997b. The list of sources is called the References list. Varying slightly from MLA style, the reference list for the Author/Date System presents the author's name and then the date of publication with other information following. Consult the APA style manual for further details.

A final note on documentation styles: regardless of the system you use, your documentation must be concise and accurate. Although many professors may not specify a style, this does not mean that they will accept any careless, inconsistent attempt to identify sources. To avoid problems, select a style and use it accurately.

For different documentation styles, consult other guides. The names and publication information of several style manuals are listed below:

### Biology
*CBE Style Manual: A Guide for Authors, Editors, and Publishers in the Biological Sciences*
Published by the Council of Biology Editors

**Chemistry**
*Handbook for Authors of Papers in American Chemical Society Publications*
Published by the American Chemical Society

**Mathematics**
*A Manual for Authors of Mathematical Papers*
Published by the American Mathematical Society

**Psychology**
*Publication Manual of the American Psychological Association*
Published by the American Psychological Association


## ACKNOWLEDGING SOURCES

As you know, when using information from outside sources, you must acknowledge the sources. This means that you must include information about the source in your paper and in the list of references. That is, you must identify where you got the information you used as a direct quotation or as a paraphrase. The following example of properly acknowledged source material includes a citation containing the author's name and page number. (The citation is also called a parenthetical reference.)

> Praising Margaret Mead, the widely acclaimed anthropologist, one author concludes, "In a world where many are famous for no special good reason or for dubious deeds, Margaret Mead, all her nearly seventy-seven years, not only attracted but deserved the attention of the public" (Howard 444).
>
>                              Author   Page


## COMMON KNOWLEDGE (GENERAL KNOWLEDGE)

When writing a research paper, you probably will use material known as "common knowledge" or "general knowledge." This type of information may be known by most educated people or may be commonly available in general sources—popular books, most dictionaries, newspapers, or magazines. You may use common knowledge without providing documentation. Review these examples of common knowledge:

- AIDS presents serious concerns for health care workers.
- Cigarettes produce hazardous second-hand smoke.
- The Greek philosopher Aristotle wrote *Poetics*, history's most influential work of literary criticism.
- Darwin's theory of natural selection holds that the species of plants and animals which survive are those best adapted to the environment.
- A disparity exists between the annual earnings of skilled and unskilled workers.

Consider these questions when trying to determine if your material is general knowledge: Did you know the information or did you have to look it up? Will your readers know this information? Is this information readily available in other sources?

If your material is not general knowledge, you must cite your source or sources. This means that you must provide a citation identifying where you found your information. If you cannot determine if your information is common knowledge, provide a citation because it's best to be cautious when using sources. Review the following section on plagiarism to avoid problems with citing sources.

## PLAGIARISM AND RESEARCH ETHICS

*Plagiarism*—a form of academic dishonesty—is the incorrect use of information from a source. This offense occurs when a writer uses another person's wording and/or ideas without correct mention of the source. Since an author's work is protected by law, the misuse of another's material is not viewed lightly. Academic policies generally provide serious consequences for plagiarism.

Documenting (also known as acknowledging sources or providing citations) means giving credit to the author of your source. When you fail to mention your source, you lead your reader to believe that the ideas and wording are your own. Simply stated, plagiarism is cheating. Instructors have little difficulty detecting plagiarism because writing styles differ; your style does not match that of your sources.

The most obvious form of plagiarism is the blatant copying of information without enclosing it in quotation marks and without providing appropriate documentation. However, unintentional plagiarism often occurs when source material is used carelessly. Paraphrased material that depends too heavily on the author's wording and sentence structure (as explained in the later section titled "Accuracy in Paraphrasing," pages 64–65 of this manual) constitutes plagiarism even though you cite the source. To avoid problems with plagiarism, follow these guidelines:

**1.** Take notes carefully when using sources. Use quotation marks to indicate material taken word-for-word from a source. Copy the information accurately. Give attention to every word, however insignificant it may seem. To avoid confusion, keep your information from sources separate from notes expressing your own views on the topic.

**2.** Use quotation marks if you take three or more consecutive words from a source. Review the section titled "Using Direct Quotations," pages 61–62 for more information.

**3.** Rewrite the original in your own style. If you wish to paraphrase, replace the author's words with your own and remember to provide a citation in your paper. A simple rearrangement of phrases is not an acceptable paraphrase.

**4.** When reviewing your finished paper, check for the accurate use of borrowed material. The reader should be able to differentiate between your ideas and those from other sources.

**5.** Provide complete and accurate information in your reference list (called Works Cited) for all sources, whether they are books, periodicals, audiovisual materials, surveys, class lectures, or interviews. Remember to document all information that is not your own, unless it is common knowledge. *If you are uncertain as to whether documentation is necessary, provide the citation to avoid problems.*

## USING ELECTRONIC SOURCES APPROPRIATELY

Instructors are very aware of the fact that the electronic transfer of data enables students to procure information from a variety of sources. In fact, they know that it is possible to copy an entire page of information from an Internet source and place it in a research paper. As a student research writer, you should know that it's wrong to take information from a source, even if it's an Internet source, if you have not provided appropriate documentation. Furthermore, copying an entire page or even a complete paragraph is unacceptable. Instructors trust you to be careful about using sources, emphasizing that you must (1) select suitable sources, (2) use the information appropriately, and (3) acknowledge where you located the source.

Other forms of academic dishonesty involve "loaning" your paper or part of your paper to another student. You are guilty of cheating if you allow someone else to use your work, whether it be to copy your computer disk or to use your sources. The best advice is to do your own work and to expect others to do likewise.

## TECHNIQUES FOR USING SOURCE MATERIAL

### General Guidelines

When taking information from outside sources, you may use the following techniques to incorporate that material into your paper:

**Quotation:** Using the information word-for-word as it appears in the original. This technique is most effective when the number of direct quotations is limited and when only brief sections of select passages are quoted. Use quotation marks when taking three or more consecutive words from the original. A quotation requires documentation.

**Paraphrase:** Putting the information into your own words while retaining the main idea and some key words; changing the word order and sentence structure. This technique is used when detailed information from a specific passage is needed. The paraphrase requires documentation.

**Summary:** Writing the main idea of a lengthy selection in your own words; condensing large amounts of material for the purpose of focusing only on major points. This technique is commonly used for article summaries and book reviews. Documentation is required.

Incorporate each of these techniques into your paper. For detailed explanations and examples of these three techniques, review the following sections.

***Using Direct Quotations***    *Quoting* means using the exact wording of the source and giving credit by presenting information about the source. Many student writers fail to understand the proper use of quotations. Pulling randomly selected blocks of information from a source and tossing them into a paper as direct quotations creates a poor product. Stringing together several pieces of information in a "cut-and-paste" manner also reveals inexperience. Avoid these incorrect approaches by being selective when choosing material to quote and by limiting your use of direct quotations. For an accurate and effective use of quotations, follow these guidelines:

> Use a quotation only when the material is extremely complex or particularly well worded, or when your reworded version lessens the impact of the original statement.
>
> Use quotations for definitions, main concepts, explanations, and narrations. However, avoid using too much quoted material because it creates a stiff, ineffective style.
>
> Analyze the material before you insert it as a direct quotation. You might have discovered some vital facts, but unless the author presents them in an exceptional manner, do not use them in a direct quotation. Using a paraphrase is more appropriate.

Although many student research papers are filled with one quotation after the next, instructors prefer that students paraphrase source material because this technique requires students to think about the material. A good rule to follow is *paraphrase more and quote less.*

***Incorporating Quotations Effectively***    When you have selected material appropriate for quoting, try to avoid "dropping" the quotation into place. That is, quoted material should be woven into your writing, with attention given to clarity and smoothness. Incorporating quotations—a process inexperienced writers often fail to employ—takes time and skill.

Quotations can be integrated into your paper in a number of ways. Review the following examples, noticing that in all cases the quoted material makes up only part of a sentence. That is, a quotation should not stand alone as a separate sentence. Some type of introductory wording should be used with a direct quotation. Note the correct placement of the citations in the following examples:

> A. "Psychotherapy can be defined in terms of two sets of behaviors and intentions," according to I. H. Paul, the noted professor of psychology, "those of the therapist and those of the patient" (7).

> B. In *The Form and Technique of Psychotherapy*, Paul states, "Psychotherapy can be defined in terms of two sets of behaviors and intentions, those of the therapist and those of the patient" (7).
>
>        No Period Here      Period at End

> C. Psychotherapy, as described by an expert in the field of clinical psychology, is defined "in terms of two sets of behaviors and intentions, those of the therapist and those of the patient" (Paul 7).

D. "Psychotherapy," explains Paul in *The Form and Technique of Psychotherapy*, "can be defined in terms of two sets of behaviors and intentions, those of the therapist and those of the patient" (7).

E. "Psychotherapy can be defined in terms of two sets of behaviors and intentions, those of the therapist and those of the patient," writes Paul (7).

Options A and E identify the author in the body of the text, thus adding a smooth flow. In addition, the information about the author adds credibility to the author as a valid source and to you as a conscientious researcher. For variety, insert the identifying phrase at the end or in the middle of the quoted material as shown in examples A, D, and E. All examples consist of single sentences, a construction used to eliminate confusion for the reader. Note that when the author's name appears in the text, it is not included in the citation with the page number.

Use a colon to introduce a quotation when you attach the quotation to an already completed sentence. Usually the colon introduces a long quotation. For additional information, see the section titled "Colon" (page 116) in this manual.

***Lead-In Words to Introduce Quotations***   To skillfully integrate the quotation into your text, appropriate wording is necessary. Some commonly used lead-in words are listed below:

| | | |
|---|---|---|
| analyzes | demonstrates | indicates |
| suggests | argues | examines |
| lists | summarizes | cites |
| explores | notes | concludes |
| finds | reports | considers |
| identifies | shows | |

Review the following examples, noticing how present tense verbs are used to introduce source material:

In his article "Anti-fur Groups Wage War Against Mink Ranches," James Brooke examines the philosophy and activities of the Animal Liberation Front. He notes that the FBI classifies this group as a "domestic terrorist organization" because they have raided twenty-two mink farms over the last year and caused millions of dollars of damage (A22).

Alfred and Emily Glossbrenner, authors of *Internet 101: A College Student's Guide*, analyze the use of Internet reference resources. They conclude that these valuable resources are best used with a fast hard drive and a four-speed CD-ROM drive (226).

## Verb Tense

Present tense verbs are used to introduce material from a source. You may alter the verb tense of a quotation if the form is not consistent with that of your own wording. Use square brackets, not parentheses, to indicate this change as shown:

Discussing the 1998 policy on airline overbooking compensation, Carter <u>notes</u> that "the guidelines [promoted] a better understanding with the customers" (8).

The section titled "Brackets" (page 115 of this manual) further explains the use of brackets to indicate a change in the original.

### Accuracy in Quoting

Quotations must be an accurate reproduction of the source. Copy material from the original carefully when using a quotation. Since you are not the author of the original, you are not permitted to make any changes—even changes in grammar and spelling—without using brackets or ellipses to indicate such alteration. You may make capitalization changes, however, without using brackets. (See "Capitalization in Quoted Material" on pages 115–16 for examples.)

Be accurate with the wording, spelling, and punctuation as reviewed in the following samples from Isaac Asimov's "Beyond the Night Sky." The errors in this quotation resulted from careless copying of the original.

#### Original

There are stars that pulsate continuously in a great cosmic breathing, and others that, having consumed their fuel, expand and redden until they swallow up any planets that may orbit them.

#### Inaccurate Quotation

"There are stars that pulsate continuously and others that having consumed their fuel, expand until they swallow up any planets that orbit," says Asimov (178).

#### Accurate Quotation

In "Beyond the Night Sky," scientist Issac Asimov writes that some stars "pulsate continuously in a great cosmic breathing, and others that, having consumed their fuel, expand and redden until they swallow up any planets that may orbit them" (178).

### Using Paraphrases

*Paraphrasing*, the rewriting of an author's material into your own words, requires time and effort. Instructors prefer that you paraphrase, rather than directly quote, your source material because the flow of information will be smoother, creating less distraction for the reader. Through paraphrasing, you can also eliminate any wordiness or confusion that appears in the original. In addition, you will become more familiar with the content when you have to work on the wording of a paraphrase as opposed to just "tossing in" a direct quotation. To accurately paraphrase, follow these steps:

1. Read the selected passage carefully, being certain that you understand it. To eliminate the copying of words from the original, try to work from memory and avoid looking at the passage while paraphrasing the information.

2. Rewrite the information into a statement of main idea and relevant details, preserving the exact meaning of the original.

3. Analyze the key words and determine which to use and which to omit.

4. Replace other words with synonyms. Use a dictionary or thesaurus to help you locate appropriate synonyms, being careful to select words that do not change the meaning of the original.

5. Construct a new word order. Remember to include an introductory statement so the paraphrase blends smoothly into the text of your paper.

6. Include a parenthetical reference to the source, but do not use quotation marks.

7. Check for clarity, accuracy, and originality.

***Accuracy in Paraphrasing***   When writing a paraphrase, you may use some words from the original without quotation marks. For example, you may use proper nouns, technical terms, and some simple wording from your source. However, quotation marks are needed for distinct, original wording, even if it's only three or four words. Remember that using extensive wording (three or more consecutive words) from the original requires the use of quotation marks.

To emphasize, *a paraphrase always requires a citation.* Some students become confused about this, believing that a citation isn't necessary when paraphrasing because the exact wording was not quoted. This is incorrect, because you must identify where you got the ideas even if you don't use the exact wording of the original. If you paraphrase the author's information and don't provide a citation, you are guilty of plagiarism. To avoid problems with academic dishonesty remember to include a citation with your paraphrases.

To better understand paraphrasing, study the following example from *A History of England* by Roberts and Roberts. The original is presented first, followed by a correct and an incorrect paraphrase:

### Original

The Elizabethans also lost substantial sums in efforts to plant colonies abroad, but from these endeavors the English learned lessons that were later to pay rich dividends.

### Correct Paraphrase

In *A History of England*, Roberts and Roberts indicate that although the Elizabethans suffered financially, the attempts to colonize abroad provided valuable lessons (300).

### Incorrect Paraphrase

The Elizabethans lost substantial sums of money when trying to colonize, but from these ventures they learned lessons that were later to pay rich dividends (Roberts and Roberts 300).

Even though the source is cited, the Roberts and Roberts paraphrase is not correct. In fact, this sample is a form of plagiarism because the writer relies too heavily on the original wording. Note that the phrases "lost substantial sums" and "learned lessons that were later to pay rich dividends" were copied from the original and used without quotation marks. Examine the original again, noting that an acceptable paraphrase avoids the overuse of wording from the original.

If paraphrasing is difficult because you cannot find synonyms for the original wording, you may want to combine a paraphrase with a quotation. This technique is described in the next section.

When paraphrasing, do not include your own ideas along with those of the source. Change only the form, not the content, of the passage. Also remember that paraphrasing does not mean that you are trying to condense the original. The lengths of a paraphrase and the original version often are the same. For some passages, however, the paraphrase is briefer. If you are trying to condense the original, use the technique of summarizing, which is described in the next section.

Paraphrasing is a method for using source material that helps you avoid using too many quotations in your paper. As mentioned earlier, instructors prefer paraphrasing because this writing technique requires you to analyze the meaning of a passage and then present the information in your own words. Further, the flow of information is smoother if you use a paraphrase rather than a quotation. Avoid plagiarism by wording your paraphrases carefully and by citing the source. Remember to use quotation marks if you use three or more consecutive words from the original.

**Paraphrasing Exercise**

### Program to Help Keep Kids Safe on Internet

In an effort to curtail the spread of child pornography over the Internet, a group of government, computer industry, and advocacy group leaders announced a high-tech tip line parents can use to report those who may be preying on kids.

The CyberTipline, which will be run by the nonprofit National Center for Missing and Exploited Children and could be activated within months, will allow parents to report suspicious activity by filling out an online form or by calling a toll-free number. The center will process and forward all tips to such law enforcement agencies as the FBI and the U.S. Customs Service.

The CyberTipline is the newest of many weapons law enforcement agencies are wielding against lawbreakers on the Internet, said FBI Director Louis Freeh, who is scheduled to testify before a Senate appropriations subcommittee on the development of a $10 million FBI program aimed at combating Internet users who exploit children.

America Online, Sun Microsystems, and others are donating the technology to run the hot line, and private industry is footing half of the $600,000 bill. Several European countries have had similar tip lines for more than a year. The hotline in England said it received 781 reports during 1997 and was able to remove 2,000 pornographic images of children from the Internet.

_____

_____

_____

_____

_____

_____

_____

_____

_____

_____

_____

_____

_____

_____

## Combining a Quotation and a Paraphrase

You may use a quotation and a paraphrase in the same sentence if the information is from the same source. Quote a limited amount of significant wording and paraphrase the remainder. Make sure that your reader is able to tell where the source material begins and ends as shown in the following passage:

> Social historians have developed new methods for achieving "the silent, mathematical resurrection" of the past (5).

At times you will need to use the style of combining a quotation and a paraphrase when presenting several sentences of information from your source. Follow the style shown below, being careful to indicate where the source material begins and ends:

> The fight against teen pregnancy has taken a new direction. According to David Diamond, author of "When Having Babies Is A Crime," new federal welfare reform legislation requires states to enforce laws which prohibit sex between adults and minors as well as between minors and minors. Designed to "impose punitive approaches to convince people to change their reproductive behavior," this provision seeks to charge pregnant teens and their boyfriends with sex-related crimes such as

fornication, a misdemeanor which brings a fine of $300 and up to six months of jail (18). This means that a seventeen-year-old boy who has consensual sex with his sixteen-year-old girlfriend can be charged with statutory rape.

## Writing Summaries

To present the general idea from a long passage, use a summary. Focus on the major points and omit details and examples. When preparing a summary, read the source carefully and locate the main ideas. Usually the topic sentences, headings, and key words contain the most important information. When writing a summary, you must accurately and briefly state the main ideas in your own words.

Summarizing requires skillful wording. Present the author's ideas in your own words, but do not copy the author's exact wording. You may, however, use select words, such as proper nouns, technical terms, or simple wording without documentation. Remember that if you use three or more consecutive words from the original, you must use quotation marks.

The following sample, based on a passage from an article in the *Florida Bar Journal* titled "Bench/Bar Relationship" by John F. Harkness, demonstrates a summary. Even though the author's wording is not used, documentation is required for a summary. Compare the length of the original to that of the summary.

### Original

The partnership between the bench and the Bar should never be forgotten. Only through cooperation and mutual concern can the problems which face the justice system in the future be handled. If you remember the figures in a recent newspaper article, Florida will be the third largest state in the country by the year 2000. Our population will almost double. That could mean basically doubling everything about our system. The bench and the Bar must stand together to be able to answer the predicted and the unforeseen problems.

### Summary

Harkness suggests that judges and attorneys cooperate to manage the problems confronting the rapidly growing state of Florida (594).

Remember that your summary should be a *brief* condensation of the original. The paragraph from the original shown above contains eighty-seven words, whereas the summary uses only eighteen words. Furthermore, the summary repeats only three words from the original. Notice that synonyms are used frequently. For example, the wording "judges and attorneys" replaces "bench and the Bar."

Inexperienced student writers often fail to summarize information from their sources. Because they do not know how to manage large amounts of information, they tend to copy long paragraphs from a source and drop them into the paper in the form of direct quotations. To avoid the poor products that are created by this careless technique, learn how to use paraphrases and summaries in your research writing.

When used correctly, summarizing is a very useful technique for presenting information from sources. It is particularly useful when you need to use a significant amount of information from one source.

## Guidelines for Avoiding Plagiarism

- Do I understand the difference between common knowledge (which doesn't need to be cited) and information from sources that needs to be cited?
- Is my paraphrasing accurate? Have I avoided copying three or more consecutive words from the original? Are the paraphrases cited?
- Are my direct quotations exact reproductions of the original wording? Are the quotations cited?
- Does my Works Cited list include all of the sources I used in the paper? Is the source information recorded accurately?

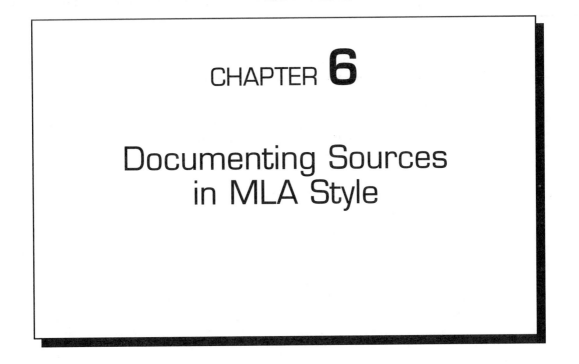

CHAPTER **6**

# Documenting Sources in MLA Style

## ACKNOWLEDGING SOURCES

Every borrowed sentence or idea requires a citation. Failure to give credit to an outside source when you paraphrase, quote, or summarize is a serious academic offense, as noted earlier. When using an author's words or ideas, acknowledge the source. *Acknowledging the source* means presenting documentation that tells where you found the information. Documentation helps the reader locate the sources you consulted, thus identifying you as a credible research writer.

Your system of giving information about a source must follow a standard pattern. Inserting a *citation* (also known as a *parenthetical reference*) within the text of your paper is the most practical way to key the information about a source to a reference list included with your paper.

This chapter presents examples of documentation according to Modern Language Association (MLA) style. For American Psychological Association (APA) documentation, refer to Chapter 12.

Lengthy citations and nonstandard forms confuse your readers, so provide brief, accurate information. Citations should be used as needed and should contain only the information necessary for identifying the source on the reference list. The citation generally includes the author's last name and the page number, as shown below:

When compared to the short story, the novel contains more social and historical complexity (Hall 195).

　　　　　　Author　Page
　　　　　　No Comma　　Period After Parentheses

To punctuate the citation, place a period after the information in parentheses. Note that a comma *does not* separate the author's name and the page number according to MLA documentation style.

When using sources, remember that the parenthetical reference is designed to help the reader locate full bibliographic information in the Works Cited. Be concise and accurate with both the citation and the Works Cited entry. Note this sample entry for the Hall book:

> Hall, Donald. <u>To Read Literature: Fiction, Poetry, Drama</u>.
> New York: Holt, Rinehart and Winston, 1997.

## PREPARING THE CITATION (PARENTHETICAL REFERENCE)

When preparing a citation, remember that a relationship exists between information given in the text and information enclosed in parentheses. For example, if you include an author's name in the text, do not repeat it in the citation. When citing an entire work, the preferred style is to include the author's name in the text.

Review the following examples, noting the correct placement of quotation marks, parenthetical references, and periods:

**1.   Author's Name in Text: Direct Quotation**
A significant point, as Hall writes, is that "a poem's tone reveals the writer's attitude toward the subject" (427).

**2.   Author's Name in Text: Paraphrase**
Hall notes that the novel's length requires a complex structure (195).

**3.   Author's Name in Citation: Direct Quotation**
An experienced reader understands characterization and identifies various types. For example, in most short stories, "a round character is dynamic or changing" (Hall 40).

**4.   Author's Name in Citation: Paraphrase**
Reading literature is a learned ability, something that requires practice and effort (Hall vi).

**5.   Name of Author and Source in Text**
In <u>To Read Literature: Poetry, Drama, and Fiction</u>, Hall describes stereotypes as being thoroughly predictable, undeveloped stock characters (48).

## LINKING SEVERAL SENTENCES BASED ON ONE SOURCE

You may use one citation to present several sentences of information paraphrased from one source. Signal the reader that the material in these sentences came from the same source by using transitional devices such as repeated key words and pronoun reference. To be most effective, present information about the author and the source first. Follow with other sentences that refer to the author. This means that you will have to use wording that clearly identifies that your information is from one source.

Review the following sample paragraph from a student paper titled "Today's Crisis in Education." Notice in the example below that four sentences are based on information from Nan Stone, author of "Does Business Have Any Business in Education?" in *Harvard Business Review*. Because the second, third, and fourth sentences are linked to the first, only one citation is needed. Note that the citation lists pages 46 through 52, thus indicating that the information was paraphrased from several pages of Stone's article.

> Problems in education have a negative impact on American business. In a recent Harvard Business Review article, management specialist Nan Stone describes the interrelationship between the classroom and the workplace. She notes that in today's competitive environment, American companies will not prosper without a steady supply of educated, motivated, disciplined young people. These companies cannot rely on new technology or promote self-managed teams if the employees are not competent and reliable. Stone concludes that the economic marketplace will suffer because American students can memorize facts but cannot analyze or interpret the information (46–52). As evident, the problems of the classroom extend into the business world. Educators and business executives must recognize that a strong economy depends on a solid educational system.

The first use of an author's name should include both the first and last names and some brief information about the author. Use the last name only for all subsequent references to that author.

## USING INDIRECT (SECONDARY) SOURCES

If possible, use information from an original source, also known as a primary source. At times, however, only an indirect or secondary source is available.

When an article or book presents facts from another source, you must acknowledge that primary source if you want to use the information. This means that you must cite the source you used to find the information and mention where the information first appeared. Review this example, noting that the Works Cited entry lists the secondary source.

> In Civilization Before Greece and Rome, H. W. Saggs describes the work of Otto Neugebauer, a distinguished historian of science who investigated the impact of the early Egyptian civil calendar. Neugebauer's research reveals that this calendar is the basis for the Gregorian calendar used today (232–33).

**Works Cited**

Saggs, H. W. Civilization Before Greece and Rome. New Haven: Yale University
Press, 1997.

An indirect source may be a publication containing a direct quotation from another person. When quoting or paraphrasing a quotation from another source, you must acknowledge who said the words and identify the source in which the quotation first appeared. Use "qtd. in" (quoted in) when citing the indirect source.

The examples shown below are based on an article by Robin Wilson. In the article, Wilson presents a direct quotation from Nadine Strossen. To use the Strossen quotation in a paper, either as a quotation (as shown in Example A) or as a paraphrase (as shown in Example B), include the notation "qtd. in" in your citation:

### *EXAMPLE A: DIRECT QUOTATION*

As President of the American Civil Liberties Union (ACLU), Nadine Strossen claims that college policies to stop racist and sexist speech are ineffective. She states, "I am so convinced the appropriate response is education and not discipline" (qtd. in Wilson: A5).

### *EXAMPLE B: PARAPHRASE*

Nadine Strossen, former President of the American Civil Liberties Union (ACLU) believes that education is the appropriate position against hate-speech (qtd. in Wilson: A5).

**Works Cited**

Wilson, Robin. "She Goes Wherever Civil Rights are Threatened." <u>Chronicle of Higher Education</u> 18 March 1995: A5.

## USING DIFFERENT SOURCES WITHIN THE SAME PARAGRAPH

Incorporating two or more sources into the same paragraph requires skillful writing. To determine if information from more than one source belongs in the same paragraph, analyze your material. Does the information from each source support the same main point? If the material is closely related, work it into one paragraph. Construct a carefully worded topic sentence and present information from the first source. To serve as a transition, use an inference between the information from the first source and that from a second source.

### *EXAMPLE A: CASINO GAMBLING*

Casino gambling should not be legal because it has negative socioeconomic effects. Law enforcement officials recognize that legalized gambling brings crime into a city. For example, Atlantic City experienced a four hundred percent increase in larceny and a one hundred and thirty-eight percent increase in violent crimes such as rape and robbery (Kelley 18). When gambling is legalized, citizens must pay for the increased costs to the judicial system. An article in <u>Criminal Law Bulletin</u> reports that residents of Illinois must pay over $200 dollars more per year in state taxes to cover the costs of law enforcement and criminal justice (Kindt 11). Making citizens subsidize gambling is unreasonable, considering that the tax money could be put to better use by improving schools or by providing better public services.

### *EXAMPLE B: INDECENCY ON THE INTERNET*

A cyberwar is waging between free speech advocates and social conservatives regarding indecent materials available to children through the Internet. The issue has become complex, going beyond just the moral matter of exposing young people to online pornography. According to Donna Rice Hughes, communications director of "Enough is Enough," a nonprofit organization against x-rated Internet carriers, Internet porn is a thriving business. She writes, "Porn-based Web sites are the third largest source of revenue on the Net" (16). This reveals that pornographers have found a profitable new delivery system. The problem, of course, is regulating who has access to the materials. The Supreme Court is reviewing arguments about the constitutionality of the Communications Decency Act which makes it illegal to provide indecent materials to minors through the Internet (Gallagher 6A). This debate reflects our view of the value of children in society. Reasonable safeguards protecting children are needed even though they may cause the Internet porn business to be regulated by the government.

Provide a smooth flow from one point to the next, accurately documenting each source. However, do not combine quoted material from one source with para-phrased material from another source in the same sentence because this confuses the reader.

## PLACING THE CITATION

Internal documentation should not disrupt your content, so keep your citations brief. Poorly placed citations break the flow of your sentences and cause problems for your readers. For best results, place the citation (1) near the material being documented, (2) at the end of the sentence, or (3) at a natural pause in the sentence. Remember these basics when preparing citations:

- If you give the author's name in the text, do not repeat it in the citation.
- If an author's name is not given, use a shortened version of the title for the citation.
- If the article is one page in length, you may omit the page number in the citation. This means that *no* parenthetical reference is needed if you use the author's name in the text.
- If using information from an alphabetically arranged source (such as an encyclopedia), you may omit the page number.

Refer to the following sections for additional information on documenting sources.

## PROBLEMS IN DOCUMENTING SOURCES

### No Author Given

When a source does not give an author's name, cite the work by shortened title. For example, the article titled "Disease Makes Pariahs of Yellowstone's Bison" would be shortened to "Disease."

Omit the page number in the citation for one-page articles, dictionaries or ency-clopedias, and nonprint sources.

For the reference list, alphabetize the source by title. Omit "A," "An," and "The" when used as the first word in the title. You may omit the page and volume numbers if a source—such as a dictionary or encyclopedia—presents articles alphabetically. These examples are keyed to the sample Works Cited that follows:

> State and federal agencies are investigating the fate of the bison in Yellowstone National Park ("Disease").
>
> The FDA has developed a priority drug approval system which allows the agency to expedite the review process for drugs which "represent a significant advance in medical treatment" ("FDA" 38).
>
> Michelangelo's Pieta, according to the Encyclopedia Americana, expresses the artist's belief that reality can be disregarded ("Michelangelo").
>
> Compact computer memories are available on flash cards the size of credit cards, storing 20 megabytes of information ("Technology").
>
> Since consumers learned of electromagnetic fields, they have started to question the safety of electric blankets ("Warmth" 31).
>
> Surveys of college graduates reveal that strong communication skills are essential to success in a career ("Students").

### Works Cited

"Disease Makes Pariahs of Yellowstone's Bison." <u>National Geographic</u> Jan. 1998: 141.

"FDA Reform Issues; Approval Process, Data Requirements, Information Dissemination." <u>Congressional Digest</u> 76.2 (1997): 38-9.

"Michelangelo." <u>Encyclopedia Americana</u>. 1996 ed.

"Students Discover the Basics: Good Communication is Essential." <u>Chronicle of Higher Education</u> 29 Feb. 1996: B8.

"Technology on Display." <u>Megabyte</u> Jan. 1997: 26.

"Warmth: Are You Going to Pay a High Price?" <u>Consumer Newsletter</u> March 1997: 17+.

If the page numbers are not consecutive, use a "+" to indicate that additional pages were used. That is, if the article begins on page 16 and continues on pages 19 and 20, use the notation "16+."

Abbreviate the names of all months except May, June, and July.

## Two Works by Same Author

When citing two or more works by the same author, include the author's name, a shortened form of the title, and the page number. Use a comma to separate the author's name from the title, but do not insert a comma between the title and page, as shown in the first example below.

Note variations if the author's name or the title is used in the text. Remember that if the author's name is used in the sentence, it should not be repeated in the citation. The *Washington Post Magazine* columnist Richard Cohen is the author of both articles mentioned in these examples:

> In "Chances of a Lifetime" Cohen notes that having fun was more enjoyable before "science took the fun out of smoking, drinking and other bad habits" (8).

> Even for those who were raised with paper and pencil, the Internet has become a great way to access knowledge (Cohen, "Screen").

Comma   No page<br>number for one-<br>page article

> In his *Washington Post Magazine* article, author Richard Cohen explores man's search for happiness and control ("Chances" 8).

No Comma

**Works Cited**

Cohen, Richard. "Chances of a Lifetime." <u>Washington Post Magazine</u> 7 Jan. 1997:
   8,10.
———. "Screen Test." <u>Washington Post Magazine</u> 21 Dec. 1996: 6.

## More Than One Author

If the source you use has two or three authors or editors, list each one. You may give the last names of all the authors in the citation and in the Works Cited, or you may give one last name followed by the Latin "et al." which means "and others." Use the style for "et al." only if the source has more than three authors.

When listing the authors' names, use the order in which the names are given on the title page, even though they may not be in alphabetical order. The following samples demonstrate works by more than one author:

> Through empowerment and consciousness-raising, today's nurse is a professional who is no longer a subservient care-giver (Mason, Backer, and Georges 97).

> Psychologists recognize that stressful situations can create both negative as well as positive influences (Benson et al. 171).

No Comma

> Geography links human society with the natural environment (DeBlij and Muller vi).

The arrangement of information for the Works Cited entry for a work by multiple authors is the same as that for a single-author publication. Give attention, however, to the style for listing authors' names.

### *TWO AUTHORS:*

DeBlij, H.J., and Peter O. Muller. <u>Geography: Regions and Concepts</u>. 7th ed. New
   York: Wiley, 1996.

**THREE AUTHORS:**

Mason, Diana J., Barbara A. Backer, and C. Alicia Georges. "Toward a Feminist
    Model for the Political Empowerment of Nurses." Image: Journal of Nursing
    Scholarship 37.4 (1995): 97–9.

pages 97 through 99

**MORE THAN THREE AUTHORS:**

Benson, Jane, et al. "Stress Reduction and the Power of Positive Thinking." Journal of
    Personality and Social Psychology 63.9 (1997) 163-91.

CHAPTER **7**

# Preparing
# an MLA
# Works Cited List

All sources contributing ideas or wording to your paper must be listed in the Works
Cited. Note that this reference list includes not only books and periodicals, but also
electronic sources and various nonprint sources such as tapes, films, and interviews.
This list contains only sources referred to in your paper.

Some students prepare a second reference list titled Works Consulted to provide
a listing of the sources they read and consulted but did not cite in the paper. Remember to prepare your reference list according to the standard forms given in this manual.

List the Works Cited entries on a separate sheet in alphabetical order according
to the author's last name. If the author's name is unknown, use the first word(s) of the
title. Remember to disregard "A," "An," or "The" from the title when alphabetizing.
See the section titled "No Author Given" on pages 73–74.

The first word in the entry should correspond to the information in the parenthetical reference. Allow the reader to easily connect the information in your text with
the source listed in the Works Cited. The sample entries presented in this publication
follow the MLA style. Additional information on typing the Works Cited List is presented in Chapter 9.

## CAPITALIZATION OF TITLES

Note that capitalization of book titles and titles of articles can be confusing. Refer to
the title page, not the cover, when looking for the title of the book. Use standard cap-

italization—capitalize first and last words and all other major words. When an article (a, an, the) appears in the middle of a title as in *All the King's Men*, do not capitalize the article. Do not use nonstandard typographical characteristics such as all capital letters or all lower case letters even though an unusual style may have been used on a book's cover.

Capitalize the title of a newspaper article or a journal article even though this style was not used in the publication. If a work has a subtitle, use a colon and a space to separate it from the title. Note this example:

The Mother Tongue: English and How It Got That Way

## WORKS CITED ENTRIES FOR PRINT SOURCES

### Book by a Single Author

The Works Cited entry for a book by one author consists basically of three parts: author, title, and publication information. Note that the publisher's name is shortened. For example, use Random for Random House, Inc., and Simon for Simon & Schuster, Inc.

At times other information such as the edition and volume is essential when citing a book. If the title page indicates an edition number, for example, provide this information in the Works Cited entry. When several copyright dates are given, use the most current date. When the names of several cities are presented, use only the first city. Follow the format presented in these examples, giving attention to the placement of information and to the punctuation:

Achebe, Chinua. Things Fall Apart. New York: Doubleday, 1994.

Nicholas, Lynn H. The Rape of Europa: The Fate of Europe's Treasures in the Third Reich and the Second World War. New York: Random, 1995.

Norton, Peter. Visual Basic for Windows. New York: Brady, 1993.

Rosenberg, Tina. The Haunted Land: Facing Europe's Ghosts After Communism. New York: Random, 1996.

### A Work in a Book or Anthology

When using a selection (short story, poem, essay, article, or chapter) from a book, begin your Works Cited entry with the author's name. Present the title of the selection in quotation marks. Use underlining for long plays (such as Romeo and Juliet) and for long poems (such as Beowulf). Give the book's title (underlined) and the editor's name, if the work has an editor. The city of publication, publisher's name, and date are then followed by a period. The final item is the page numbers, also followed by a period.

> Bloom, Alice. "On a Greek Holiday." <u>Encountering Cultures: Readings and Writings in a Changing World</u>. Ed. Richard Haleton. Boston: Blair Press, 1992. 384–94.
>
> James, Henry. "A Bundle of Letters." <u>Points of View</u>. Ed. James Moffett and Kenneth R. McElheny. New York: NAL, 1989. 79–106.

## Work Reprinted in an Anthology

If you are using a previously published essay or article, your Works Cited entry should present complete information for the earlier publication. Indicate a reprint by adding "Rpt. in."

> Anderson, Julia. "Alternative Approaches to Organizing the School Day and Year: A National Commission Examines New Structures for Improving Student Learning." <u>Journal of Reading</u> 28 (1996): 149–52. Rpt. in <u>Year-round Education: A Collection of Articles</u>. Ed. Robin Forage. Arlington Heights, IL: Skylight, 1996. 3–18.

## A Work in More Than One Volume

Present complete publication information and indicate the volume(s) used.

> Mack, Maynard, et al., eds. <u>The Continental Edition of World Masterpieces</u>. 3rd ed. 2 vols. New York: Norton, 1994.
>
> Segalat, Roger Jean. <u>How Things Work</u>. 4 vols. New York: Simon, 1996.

When preparing the citation for your paper, use the following format to cite specific pages from such a work: (8: 225–67). This notation means that you used volume 8, pages 225 through 267.

## Citing the Bible

The conventional use of quotation marks or underlining to indicate a title does not apply when citing the Bible. Present the information in the format shown below. Identify the translation used (King James Version, Oxford Annotated Edition, etc.). Other publication information is not necessary as shown in the samples below:

> Holy Bible. King James Version.
>
> Holy Bible. New Revised Standard Version.

To cite a passage from the Bible in a paper, present the book, chapter, and verse as shown below:

> (Job 38: 6–9)

## Book with a Title within a Book Title

If you use a book with a title that contains another title, note the following examples. When the book title includes the name of an essay, short story, or poem, use quotation marks around the name of the essay, short story, or poem. Underline the book's entire title. Note that the period goes before the ending quotation mark as shown in the Stewart citation.

> Stewart, Jane. <u>An Analysis of Katherine Mansfield's "The Lady's Maid.</u>" New York: American, 1994.

When a novel or play is named in a book's title, the title of the novel or play is neither underlined nor put in quotation marks. Notice that <u>The Red Badge of Courage</u> is not underlined in the title below.

> Dixler, Elsa. <u>Barron's Book Notes: Steven Crane's</u> The Red Badge of Courage. New York: Barron's, 1996.

## Encyclopedia Article, Dictionary Entry, or Article in a Reference Book

An encyclopedia article or a reference book entry is presented in the same style as a work from a book. However, the name of the reference book's author is not included. When an author's name is given, present it first. (Authors of articles in reference books often use their initials to sign their work. Look for the identification of the initials elsewhere in the book.) Remember to omit the page number when the articles in a reference book are arranged in alphabetical order.

> "Genetic Engineering." <u>World Almanac and Book of Facts</u>. 24th ed. 1995.
> "Madeleine Albright." <u>Who's Who of American Women</u>. 20th ed. 1995–96.
> "Physical Therapy and Rehabilitation." <u>Collier's Encyclopedia</u>. 1994 ed.
> "Yin and Yang." <u>Random House College Dictionary</u>. 1996 ed.

## Periodical (Article from Scholarly Journal or Magazine)

The Works Cited entry for articles from periodicals includes the author's name, title of the article, publication information, and page number(s). The title of the periodical is not followed by a period or a comma. For scholarly journals, present the volume.

Include the issue only when the pagination is not continuous from one issue to the next. Omit the issue if the publication has continuous pagination within the volume. For most scholarly journals, continuous pagination is used throughout the year. The individual issues are bound together at the end of the year, making the page numbers continuous within the annual volume.

Present the year in parentheses. Note that when using volume and/or issue numbers, use only the year and omit the month and day.

***Noncontinuous Pagination***　For periodicals with noncontinuous pagination (the page numbering system begins with page one for each issue), present the volume and issue number as shown below:

> Cooper, Edward M., and Gwynne Larsen. "Presentation Graphics Theory and Use: A Comparison of Collegiate Faculty and Industrial Graphics Users." <u>Collegiate Microcomputer</u> 10.1 (1992): 15–19.
> 　　　　　　　　　　　　　Volume　Issue

> Green, Kathleen. "Nontraditional Education: Alternative Ways to Earn Your Credentials." <u>Occupational Outlook Quarterly</u>. 40.2 (1996): 22–36.

***Continuous Pagination***　For periodicals with continuous pagination (the page numbering system does not begin with page one for each issue), present the volume number in parentheses. Do not give the issue number, as shown below:

> Allen, Arthur. "Examining Profit and Loss Statements." <u>Accounting Review</u> 71 (1995) 225–37.
> 　　　　　　　　　　　　　　　　　　　　　Volume

> Peck, Bryan T. "European Lifelong Learning Initiatives." <u>Phi Delta Kappan</u>. 77.9 (1996): 645–47.

### Bimonthly Periodical

Use the month and year rather than the volume and issue numbers. Note that parentheses around the year are omitted. Abbreviate the names of all months except May, June, and July.

> Longman, Robin. "Creating Art: Your Rx for Health." <u>American Artist</u> June 1994: 58+.
> Sololov, Raymond. "Pyramid Power." <u>Natural History</u> Jan. 1995: 72–75.

Note that "58+" indicates that the article begins on page 58 and continues on nonconsecutive pages.

## WEEKLY OR BIWEEKLY PUBLICATION OR MAGAZINE

For a weekly or biweekly publication or for a magazine, omit the volume and issue numbers and give the complete date. When the author's name is not given, begin with the title. When presenting the date, begin with the day and follow with the month and year with no intervening punctuation.

> Cheek, Dorothy and John E. Kyle. "Wingspread Takes Two-pronged Approach to Building Learning Communities: Both Local and Federal Efforts needed." <u>Nation's Cities Weekly</u> 29 Apr. 1996: 14+.
> Levy, Steven. "Microsoft vs. the World." <u>Newsweek</u> 9 Mar. 1998: 36+.

Rubin, Alissa J. and Jonathan Weisman. "Tax Cut, Minimum Wage Law."
<u>Congressional Quarterly Weekly Report</u> 21 Sept. 1996: 2795–98.

When giving the name of a periodical, omit the introductory article ("A," "An,"
or "The"). Give the name of the publication as it appears on the title page, not as it appears on the cover.

## Newspaper Article

Begin with the author's name, if given, and then present the title of the article in quotation marks. The newspaper's name appears next and is followed by the complete
date. If the paper prints different editions on a given date, specify the edition. The section and page(s) are last, preceded by a comma.

Note the correct style for the newspaper's name: give the name as it appears on
the front page and omit the introductory article "The." Provide the name of the city in
brackets if it is not included in the paper's name. No punctuation separates the newspaper's name from the date.

Use appropriate capitalization for the title of a newspaper article. According to
Modern Language Association (MLA) style, capitalize the first word and the last word
and all other principal words even though they were not capitalized in the newspaper's
headline.

Clare, Rose Marie. "Citizens Protest Closing of Jacobsen's Store." <u>Daily Sun</u>
[Dearborn, MI] 25 Feb. 1998: 8+.

No Author

"Clinton Administration Delays Acting in Case on Affirmative Action." <u>Wall Street
Journal</u> 12 Dec. 1996, western ed.: B:4.

No Punctuation      Edition   Section Pages

Nieves, Evelyn. "Casino Envy Gnaws at Falls on U.S. Side." <u>New York Times</u> 15 Dec.
1996, late ed.: 49.

## Letter to the Editor

Write "Letter" after the author's name to identify a letter to the editor.

Jones, Edward T. Letter. <u>Chronicle of Higher Education</u> 15 Jan. 1997: B12.

## Editorial

Begin with the author's name if the editorial is signed. If no author is given, present
the title first. Identify the article as an editorial and present publication information.

"Hate Crimes: Gays and Lesbians and State Laws." Editorial. <u>New York Times</u> 2 Mar.
1998, early ed.: E12.

Stroud, Joe H. "Big City or Small Town, Decay Hurts All." Editorial. <u>Detroit News</u> 15 Mar. 1998: 2H.

## Government Publication

For a government publication or a source by a corporate author, an individual author's name is not given. The work must be listed by the corporate name (i.e., United States or Carnegie Foundation) in the Works Cited. For the citation, the best style is to include the corporate name in the text of your paper as shown below:

> According to the U.S. Senate subcommittee report titled <u>Hearings on the Unemployed Worker,</u> a considerable disparity exists according to age, sex, and race (21).

The Works Cited entry for this subcommittee report appears as follows:

> United States. Senate. Subcommittee on Unemployment Compensation. <u>Hearings on the Unemployed Worker</u>. 99th Cong., 1st Session. 11, 12 Nov. 1995, 10 vols. (Washington: GPO, 1996) 121–240.

Although government and corporate publications provide valuable information for research papers, writing an accurate Words Cited entry for these materials is difficult. More specifically, you may have trouble identifying the author because often a committee or government organization prepares the publication. Further, you may have trouble finding information about the place of publication and the name of the publisher. If necessary, use the notation "n.p." (no place of publication given) as explained in the following section titled "Pamphlet."

When preparing a Works Cited entry for a government publication, focus on the most important information: title of publication, date, publication number, and page number. Since the Government Printing Office (GPO) prints most government documents, you may list GPO as the publisher if another printer is not specified. Note the following Works Cited entries:

> <u>Congressional Record</u>. 12 June 1996, D156–89.
>
> Commission on Consumer Affairs. <u>Health Hazards of Cigarette Smoking</u>. Chicago: American Bar Center, 1998.

## Pamphlet

Pamphlets follow the standard format used for a book: author, title, publication information. If a date is not given, use the notation "n.d."

Use "N.p." before the colon to indicate that no place of publication is given. If a publisher's name is not provided, use "N.p." after the colon.

> <u>Determining Your Career Choices</u>. Chicago: University of Chicago, n.d.
>
> McDonald, James and Bonnie P. Mc Donald. <u>Owning a Franchise</u>: Guaranteed Early Retirement. N.p.: BPS Printing, 1997.

## A Review

When writing a Works Cited entry for a review of a book, or play, or another work, begin with the reviewer's name and the title of the review. To indicate that your source is a review, write "Rev. of" before giving the title of the work reviewed and the author's name.

Use the format for the type of publication in which the review appears. That is, if the review is printed in a journal, follow the form for a journal article as shown below:

> Joseph, Douglas. "Expanding the Capabilities of Electronic Data Transfer." Rev. of
> <u>Data Communications, Networks and Distributed Processing</u>, by U. D. Black.
> <u>Computer Technology</u> 11 (1998) 255–61.

## DOCUMENTATION OF ELECTRONIC SOURCES

To begin, let's review some of the basics of online sources. Electronic sources contain a uniform resource locator (URL), which indicates a specific Web site. The URL presents the location or address of a computer file and therefore must be typed accurately so the source can be identified and located. This is important because the reader of your paper may want to retrieve a file to check the information you presented. Here are some of the basics:

> Be precise when typing a URL including the use of accurate spelling, punctuation, and spacing.
> A URL always appears in angle brackets < > as a means of indicating that everything within the brackets is part of the locator.
> URLs use symbols as punctuation marks as follows:
>
> | hyphen | - |
> | dot or period | . |
> | forward slash | / |
> | backslash | \ |
> | pipe | \| |
> | TILDE | ~ |
>
> To divide a URL, make the break before the punctuation mark and move the punctuation mark to the next line, as shown here:

<http://www<br>.cinema.pgh.pa.us/movie/reviews>

Here is a sample Internet address:

| Protocol (computer language for exchanging information) | Name of Domain | Directory Path |
| --- | --- | --- |

<http://www.travelweb.com/>

| Angle Bracket | Separators | Angle Bracket |
| --- | --- | --- |

## WORKS CITED ENTRIES FOR ONLINE SOURCES

Documenting electronic sources presents difficulties because firm standards have not been established. As a student researcher, you should know that documentation of many types of online sources is complex because documents are expanded, modified, and updated. In some cases, documents are deleted. Note the following areas of concern:

> **Authorship and Origin:** Some online documents do not identify an author. The origin of some sources is unknown. These factors should make you review the document carefully before deciding to use it in your paper.
>
> **Copyright:** Questions of ownership occur when using online sources. If an original has been modified, who "owns" the document?
>
> **Edition:** Once a document has been modified, has a new edition been created? The edition should be identified by date and time; the user who modified the document should be identified. Can an author prevent users from modifying a document?
>
> **Electronic Address:** Documents may be moved or located at a new address in a modified format. Can a user access a specific version of a document?

In addition to these issues, other concerns exist regarding a standard format for documenting electronic sources. An essential point to remember, however, is that the purpose of documentation is to provide information which allows readers to easily locate and access information presented in a paper.

The documentation of online materials follows the pattern used for documentation of other materials. The *MLA Handbook for Writers of Research Papers* (1995) specifies that citations in your paper identify a source by author's name and page number. The citation, of course, is keyed to an entry in the list of references known as the Works Cited list. This list provides complete bibliographic information which allows readers to locate the source. This same format is followed when documenting online materials. That is, the information in the Works Cited must enable the reader to retrieve the information from the electronic source. The documentation styles presented in this chapter for online sources follow the MLA citation principles.

### Online Databases

An online database provides access to information on the computer from an information service. Documents derived from an online database are divided into two categories:

**1.   Material that identifies publication information:** This may be a reprint of an article from any print source such as a journal government document, newspaper, or magazine. These materials are the same as the original, which was initially printed in another source. Note, however, that the pagination for the online source will not follow the original numbering.

**2. Material that does not identify a specific print source:** Some online sources, such as electronic bulletin boards and the Internet, provide information on a wide range of topics. You should avoid using informal, nondocumented sources for academic papers.

When preparing a Works Cited list, your entry should include the following items:

1. Name of the author (if given)
2. Publication information for the printed source (title and date)
3. Title of the database (underlined)
4. Publication medium (indicate "Online")
5. Name of the computer service
6. Date of access.

For some sources, you will not be able to locate all of the required information. Prepare your citation by using what is available if information is unavailable. Review the following sample Works Cited entries:

> Cotton, Paul. "Exhibit Explores Link Between Art and Epilepsy." <u>Journal of the American Medical Association</u> 272 (1994): 1887–89. <u>Infotrac: Magazine Index Plus</u>. CD-ROM. Information Access. Mar. 1997.
>
> <u>Parents in the Classroom</u>. Urbana. ERIC Clearinghouse on Elementary and Early Childhood Education. 1995, ERIC. Online. BRS. 15 Aug. 1995.
>
> Wyatt, Edward. "A Winning Formula: Forget Timing, Forget Technology." <u>New York Times</u> 28 May 1995: F6. <u>New York Times Online</u>. Online. Nexis. 7 Sept. 1995.

***Gopher Site***   A Gopher program is an easy way to connect with computer sites to retrieve information. Use the following format when documenting Internet information located through a Gopher search:

> Author's last name, first name. "Title of Document." Date of Publication. Other Print Publication Information. <URL> (Date of Access).

Sample:

> Gerard, Elmoy. "Management Problems in Small Businesses." 1997. <gopher://wiretap.bus.princ.com:mgmt>. (No date.)

***World Wide Web Site***   Begin the entry by identifying the author's name, if given. Present the title of the document in quotation marks and follow it with the title of the complete word which is underlined or in italics. Include the date of publication and the URL. The last item is the date of access which is presented in parentheses. This is the date when you located the source on the Internet. Here is the general format to follow:

Author's last name, first name. "Title of Document." <u>Title of Complete Work</u>. Date of
    Internet Publication. <URL> (Date of Access).

Review the following sample from the "Computer News Daily" of the *New York
Times* Syndicate. The information was taken from the first screen (page one) of a two
screen article.

In "Brains, Not Brawn, Drive Microsoft," author Hiawatha Bray offers comments on a
new book about Bill Gates' work in the computer software industry, noting that
Microsoft has achieved a dominant role in the Internet market (1).

Citation Lists Screen Number

### Works Cited

Bray, Hiawatha. "Brains, Not Brawn, Drive Microsoft." 14 Feb. 1997.
    <http://www.globe.com> (23 Feb. 1997).

Remember that MLA style does not require a citation for a one-page work. This
means that many online sources will not have a citation because they are single-screen
documents. It is essential, however, to use wording that tells your reader where the
source material ends.

***E-mail Messages***   Documenting e-mail requires the following information:

Author's last name, first name. <e-mail address> "Subject Line." Publication Date.
    Identification of type. (Date of Access.)

### Works Cited

Heurlin, George. <heurlingeo@icc.gate.trsco> "Open Mail." 29 Nov. 1996.
    Distribution list. (3 Dec. 1996.)
Roberts, Natalie. <natrob@bwe.bce> "Competitive Quoting." 20 Dec. 1996. Personal
    e-mail. (21 Jan. 1997.)

***Listserv Messages***   A *listserv message* is an ongoing discussion via e-mail.
Provide the following information when documenting this type of electronic communication:

Author's last name, first name. <Author's e-mail address> "Subject line." in TITLE
    LIST SITE (if known), Date of Internet Publication. <Listserv Address> (Date of
    Access.)

### Works Cited

Johnson, Carole. <johnxcc@lvcc.sf.bio.edu>, "Investigating Mineral Deficiencies in
    Diets of Elderly Samoans," in D-NUTRITION, 10 Jan. 1977.
    <d-nutrition@wgsu>, 5 Feb. 1997.
Wilson, J.J. <jjwil@smu.sci.med>, "REPLY: Dietary Studies," in D-NUTRITION,
    <d-nutrition@wgsu>, 1 Mar. 1997.

***CD-ROM (Nonperiodical Database)*** Some CD-ROM databases are issued as a single publication, not as a periodical. Follow the format used for a book and provide the publication medium. Note that a vendor's name is not included in the Works Cited entry as shown below:

> <u>Encarta: Multimedia Encyclopedia</u>. 1994 ed. CD-ROM. Redmond: Microsoft, 1994.
> "Psychosis." <u>The New Grolier Multimedia Encyclopedia</u>. 1993 ed. CD-ROM.
>     Software Toolworks, Inc. 1993.

***Computer Software*** After the standard format of author, title, and descriptive label (i.e., computer software), list other relevant information for commercially produced computer programs. Underline the title of the program.

> Lynwood, Robert. <u>Learning About Music</u>. Computer software. Computron Software of
>     Memphis, 1998.
> Stephen, Michelle. <u>Discovering Ancient Egypt</u>. Computer software. Micromax
>     Computer Services, San Francisco, 1997. Micron 2500, 8KB, disk and manual.

***Information Service Material*** If you use material from an information service, the Works Cited entry resembles that of other printed material. A reference to the service and the identification number appear at the end of the citation.

> Little, Richard. <u>Educational Programs to Reduce Teen Pregnancy</u>. ERIC, 1998. ED 122
>     8021.

## WORKS CITED ENTRIES FOR NONPRINT SOURCES

### Television and Radio Programs

The usual order is shown below. Include other pertinent information, such as the director's or narrator's name, before the network (e.g., PBS). Note that the local station, city, and date of broadcast follow. Underline the title of a television or radio program. If the title of the episode is used, it appears in quotation marks.

For transcripts of the "CBS Evening News," use the format shown below for the *CBS News Index*. Provide a title for the segment used. If no title is available, use the subject of the segment as the title. Give the date and the page number of your print copy.

>         Title of the Segment        Title of the Series
> "Space Exploration in the Next Century." <u>Planet Earth</u>. Prod. Anne Kaplan. PBS.
>     WITF, Harrisburg 28 Sept. 1997.
> "Girls Excel in Math and Science." <u>CBS Evening News</u>. From <u>CBS News Index</u>. 19
>     Feb. 1997.

## Recordings

Identify the medium (audio tape, record, or CD) after the title is given. Include other relevant information such as manufacturer, catalog number, and year of issue. Underline the title of the recording.

> Emery, Noemie. <u>Washington: A Biography</u>. Audiotape. Read by Tom West. Recorded Books, Inc., 81310, 1996.

## Videotapes, Films, and Slide Programs

Information on physical characteristics (size and length of film or number of frames) follows the date. Include other data (such as information on the writer, performer, and/or producer) after the title. Underline the title.

> <u>Exploring Tropical Rain Forests</u>. Audiotape. Prod. National Geographic Society, Vision Span Products, 1996. 38 min.
> <u>Learning the Real Estate Business</u>. Slide Program. Developed by Deborah's Realty and the Birmingham Real Estate Association, 1998. 60 slides.

## Interviews

When citing an interview that you personally conducted, begin the Works Cited entry with the name of the person you interviewed. Identify the type of interview (telephone interview or personal interview) and provide the date as shown in the following example:

> Davis, Dianne. Personal interview. 5 Apr. 1997.

Present information about the interview in your text as follows:

> A personal interview with Dianne Davis, director of the Ann Arbor Travel Connection, revealed some significant information about luxury cruises. She notes that the average age of passengers has decreased over the past ten years.

Note that if the interviewee's name is used in the text of your paper, a citation is not necessary.

## Surveys

If you conducted an informal survey and would like to incorporate the findings into your paper, use the format which follows. Begin with the name of the person conducting the survey, and then present the survey's title in quotation marks. Identify the source as a survey and tell where and when the survey was conducted. The citation in your paper should present your name because you are the author of the survey. Note this example:

The child care crisis is not limited to big cities. I recently conducted a survey of twenty-five families with preschool children in the Oakton-Vienna area and found that 55% were not satisfied with the local day-care establishments. Several parents noted that untrained workers and limited hours were problems (Ward). As this information suggests, child-care concerns exist in many communities.

### Works Cited

Your Name in Works Cited

Ward, Linda Jean. "Survey of Day Care Parents." Informal public opinion survey conducted in Oakton-Vienna, Virginia, 10 June 1997.

## Lectures

The format for lectures, speeches, and addresses should include the title of the presentation (if known) and the name of the sponsoring organization, location, and date. Use a descriptive label (i.e., classroom lecture, keynote address, community discussion, debate, etc.) if there is no title.

Daly, Marilyn. "The Muscles in the Human Body." Classroom lecture. York College of Pennsylvania. York, 1 Nov. 1997.

Binz, Joseph. "Serving the Component Parts Industry." Association of OEM Convention. Memphis, 15 May 1998.

Note that documentation styles may vary according to the desired emphasis when citing nonprint sources. For further information on the style used in this publication, consult the *MLA Handbook for Writers of Research Papers*, published by the Modern Language Association of America. For documentation according to the American Psychological Association (APA) style, refer to Chapter 12 of this manual.

# CHAPTER **8**

# Improving
# Your Style

## DEVELOPING AN EFFECTIVE INTRODUCTION

You already know that your introductory paragraph must capture the reader's attention. That's nothing new. What you may need to think about, however, is the technique you will use to develop the introduction to your paper.

Your strategy should include a few basic components: identification of the topic, information about the organizational pattern to be followed in the paper, and presentation of the thesis. These components are essential because they provide a "road map" for your readers.

The following paragraphs present different strategies for developing an introductory paragraph. Notice that the thesis statement is placed at the end of the introductory paragraph, a position which allows your general introductory material to flow into the thesis. In the same respect, the thesis will be located close to the body paragraphs, creating a sense of unity throughout the opening sections of your paper. Review these sample introductory paragraphs carefully, noting the explanations in the margins.

### *CONSTRUCT A FICTIONAL STORY*

At age forty-nine William Harris knew that his fight with AIDS would claim his life within the next eight to ten months. His greatest wish was to leave San Francisco to visit his family in Tennessee, but his savings were depleted because he resigned from his position as a marketing director after becoming too weak to work. He worried about paying his rent and about meeting the $85 copayment each week for his medication. After careful deliberation he knew that his only option was to sell his $100,000 life insurance policy to an investment company for $78,000. Although the story of William Harris is fictional, thousands of terminally ill people are confronted with the same decision Harris faced. To resolve their financial problems, many of these people participate in the growing, yet controversial, practice of viatical settlements which allows the insured to sell their death benefits at a reduced rate before their demise. Critics of this new financial practice argue that investors who buy policies are taking advantage of the terminally ill. Our legal system must pass laws to protect vulnerable citizens from greedy investors. Viatical settlements should be illegal.

Present
Thesis


## PRESENT AN ANECDOTE FROM A SOURCE

Robert and Miriam Shear of Accelerated Benefits Capital in Oak Park, Michigan manage an investment company specializing in a controversial practice. According to a *Detroit News* article, the Shears buy life insurance policies from terminally ill patients, paying the insured approximately 70 to 80 percent of the policy's value. The Shears have made life easier for hundreds of people by providing money for terminal patients and their families (Waldsmith). Government regulations should not stop investment companies from helping needy families. In fact, viatical settlements should be protected by law.

Thesis


## POSE QUESTIONS

Have you ever thought about the plight of terminally ill patients? Do you know that many worry about the financial ruin they are causing for their families? Should terminal patients have the right to enjoy their final days without worrying about the financial security of their loved ones? If you are concerned about these issues, you might be interested in the new practice for cashing in life insurance policies before the death of the insured. Many people claim that these settlements eased the stress during a family member's illness, but others note that these settlements were a legal way for investment companies to steal their insurance money. This practice, known as viatical settlements, must be regulated by the government.

Thesis


## PRESENT A QUOTATION OF SIGNIFICANCE

"Death is the only pure, beautiful conclusion of a great passion." These words of D. H. Lawrence reveal that he saw death as a natural step after life, one which should be "pure" and "beautiful" (194). In an ideal world, death would be peaceful, without the stress of earthly worries. For many terminally ill patients, however, this is not possible because their illnesses have devastated their families emotionally as well as financially. To help the ill regain their financial security, investment companies are offering viatical settlements. This practice allows patients to sell their life insurance policies so they can enjoy the cash settlement before death. This practice is designed to alleviate financial burdens and to bring some happiness to the terminally ill. Although viatical settlements are a new form of investment, patients and their families should consider this financial option.

Thesis

### *CITE STATISTICS*

A study released last year by the U.S. Center for Disease Control and Prevention indicated that the number of deaths from AIDS has stabilized and may begin decreasing. This news is surprising to viatical investment companies because they are in the business of buying the life insurance policies of terminally ill patients. In fact, recent statistics indicate that 80 percent of their customers are AIDS patients. These people receive an average of 78 percent of the value of their insurance policies (Kramer 6). The obvious questions about viatical settlements focus on the legality and ethics of this practice. To protect citizens from financial ruin, the government must regulate viatical transactions.

Thesis

### *BEGIN WITH A DEFINITION*

Viatical Settlements. That's a new term for the investment industry as well as for terminally ill patients. This technical language identifies the practice of selling a life insurance policy for reduced rates before a terminally ill patient dies. The Latin word "viatical" means "providing a gift before a journey" ("Insurers" 10). Although thousands of people have participated in these settlements, some serious issues remain unresolved. Viatical settlements should not be allowed because of ethical, financial, and legal problems.

Thesis presents organizational statement to forecast<br>the order of the developmental paragraphs

When using a definition in your paper, whether it be in the introductory paragraph or in the body, avoid the wording "Webster defines . . ." or "According to the dictionary . . ." Replace these trite statements with a more effective approach to presenting a definition as shown in the previous examples.

Avoid introductory statements which announce what you propose to do. Some wording is ineffective such as, "In this paper I plan to argue that nuclear power plants should be abolished," or "My purpose in this paper is to convince you to support your local Humane Society." If your writing supports the thesis, then it is not necessary to make proclamations about your intentions. Some reports serve as an exception to this guideline. For example, lab reports for science courses routinely begin with a statement of the purpose.

For many writers, the introductory paragraph is the last paragraph that they write. They wait until after they have written the rest of the paper because they want to check the focus of the entire paper before they write the first paragraph. If you have trouble trying to think of a way to begin your paper, follow the suggestion of writing the opening paragraph last. Remember that the introduction motivates the reader—which is your instructor in most cases—to become involved with your writing, so take the time to prepare a good introductory paragraph.

## Concluding Your Paper

Prepare a concluding paragraph that gives your paper a sense of closure. Student writers often make the mistake of summarizing the paper in the final paragraph, a strategy that is appropriate for long papers but inappropriate for college papers that are less than ten pages.

To create the sense of the finality that your paper needs, restate your thesis. In addition, use one of these strategies for the concluding paragraph:

1. Ask questions to urge the reader to think about the material you presented.
2. Present a recommendation for further study by suggesting related issues which go beyond your thesis. Be careful, however, not to introduce new topics in the conclusion.
3. Identify a solution to the problems posed by your thesis.
4. Take the reader back to the example or story you used in your introduction and offer some concluding remarks.

## UNITY AND COHERENCE

To be effective an argument paper must do more than present logical evidence to support a thesis. An argument paper must be easy to read. This means that your paper must have unity and coherence.

*Unity:* Ideas related to a central point or thesis
*Coherence:* Connections between the ideas that create a smooth flow.

To achieve unity, all of the paragraphs in your paper must relate to the thesis. This means that you will have to remind your reader of the thesis throughout the paper. Student writers often overlook this strategy, ignoring the fact that readers need to be reminded of a paper's direction. Review the sample papers in this manual to see how the authors create a sense of unity by presenting ideas related to the thesis.

To achieve coherence, all of the ideas in your paper must be connected to each other. In the same respect, the paragraphs must be connected to each other. The reader should be able to see the link between ideas.

Here are some techniques for linking sentences within a paragraph:

1. Use transitional words and phrases
2. Repeat key points or important wording
3. Repeat sentence patterns or use parallel wording
4. Use pronoun reference
5. Use synonyms for key words.

### SAMPLE PARAGRAPH

Year-round schooling offers many benefits. One obvious advantage is that academic achievement improves with an extended school year. Educational specialist Mary Lindermuth explores this fact in her article "Does Year-Round Schooling Work?" She notes that improved academic performance was measured by a Harvard University study of achievement test scores. This research reveals that students enrolled in year-round schooling perform better in reading comprehension, vocabulary development, and general mathematics than students in the traditional 180-day school year (1012). <u>These positive results</u> which reveal the <u>strengths</u> of a longer school year are evident in other studies as well. For example, the San Pedro school district in Southern California reports that attendance has improved and truancy has decreased under their new plan for year-round schooling (Jones 27). It's evident that educators must recognize the benefits of year-round schooling.

The underlined words show how pronoun reference unites the ideas in this paragraph. In addition, note that the use of the following synonyms and related wording creates coherence: advantage, benefits, positive results, strengths.

The most effective transitions come from a natural linking of the information. This type of connection creates a smooth flow, much like the movement of a conversation as it moves from one point to the next with all elements relating to a central idea. The transitional element "for example" is used in the paragraph above as a means of introducing an example.

## TRANSITIONAL TERMS

A common method of connecting ideas is through the use of transitional wording. Review this list:

**COMPARISON**

in the same respect
just as
similarly
too
also
in the same way
likewise

**EMPHASIS**

in fact
more importantly
it's evident that
absolutely
certainly
especially
positively
of course
indeed
without a doubt
primarily

**EFFECT/RESULT**

accordingly
as a consequence
as a result
thus
because of
therefore
hence
then
due to
on account of

**ADDITION/CONTINUATION**

again
also
and
along with
as well as
besides
in addition
additionally

moreover
likewise
further
furthermore
too

**CONCESSION**

even though
although
of course
granted that
considering that
after all
admittedly

**EXAMPLE/ILLUSTRATION**

for example
to illustrate that
thus
that is
such as

for instance
specifically

**EXPLANATION**

this means that
to understand the point
simply stated
in this way

**CONDITION**

although
however
even though
if
nevertheless
considering that

if that were true
in case
on condition that
provided that
given the fact that
if that were true

**SUMMARY/CONCLUSION**

in summary
to sum up
in conclusion
finally
lastly
therefore
thus

**CONTRAST/OPPOSITION**

however
by contrast
on the other hand
whereas
yet
contrary to
but
otherwise
on the contrary
critics of this view
those opposed believe
still
opposite
opposing
instead of
unlike

When attempting to achieve coherence in your paper, follow these words of warning:

1. Do not overuse transitional words. Too many transitional devices make your wording sound artificial. Your writing will lack a natural flow if you overuse transitional words.
2. Do not misuse transitional words. Be certain that you understand the type of connection you need before inserting a transitional word.

## GUIDELINES FOR INCORPORATING SOURCE MATERIAL

The use of material from other sources affects your writing style. Your wording, therefore, will have to be particularly clear and concise so that the reader can understand the relationship between your ideas and those taken from sources. Remember not to "toss" quotations into your paper. Lead into the quoted material with an appropriate introductory statement. Make your reader realize the connection between the quotation and the rest of your paper. Read the following sample paragraphs and notice the difference in style:

### PARAGRAPH 1: AN EXAMPLE OF POOR STYLE

The issue of increasing the cigarette tax remains controversial. "In the last decade, smoking by adults has declined, but the percentage of teen-agers who smoke has remained about the same ("Tobacco" 21). Some people support a higher cigarette tax to discourage smoking by young people:

> The supporters point to Canada where the percentage of smokers among older teens fell from 24 percent to 16 percent after the national excise tax was increased

from $1.50 to $2.60 during a two-year period. In California, smoking among adults declined by 17 percent in the three years after the cigarette tax took effect, according to the State Department of Health. (Sytes 14)

The Center for Disease Control and Prevention supports the increase in cigarette tax ("Tobacco" 21). People opposed to the higher tax wonder where the money will go. Opponents say legislators will simply use the money as they please ("Tobacco" 21). They point out that the $130 million to be raised by the cigarette tax in Massachusetts is to be used for a variety of health and anti-smoking programs. According to Bristow, doctors were joining with other anti-smoking advocates to push for a 25-cent tax increase ("Tobacco" 22). Smoking causes a significant percentage of home fires. "The tobacco industry is spending enormous amounts to fight against the anti-smoking groups. With millions in donations from tobacco companies, groups opposing the tax increase mounted two unsuccessful battles to challenge the Massachusetts legislation. Supporters of the higher tax have made the tobacco money the prime target of their attacks, saying it reflects the lengths to which tobacco interests will go to protect profits" (Ludlow).

### PARAGRAPH 2: AN EXAMPLE OF EFFECTIVE STYLE

The issue of increasing the cigarette tax remains controversial. Several states support a higher cigarette tax to discourage smoking by young people and to encourage adult smokers to quit. Sylvan Sytes, author of "Tobacco Industry Fights Anti-Smoking Tax Plan," notes that this increased tax reduces smoking. He reports that the percentage of older teens smoking in Canada decreased by 8 percent, from 24 to 16 percent, during the two years following the national tax increase from $1.50 to $2.60 per pack (14). Although these numbers reveal that an excise tax may decrease the number of young smokers, the issue of raising the cigarette tax presents some problems. For example, opponents of the higher tax believe that "legislators will simply use the money as they please" even though the $130 million to be raised by a cigarette tax is slated for various health programs ("Tobacco" 22). How the money will be spent certainly is a valid concern, but it's not the only issue. Another problem is the tobacco industry's fight against an increase in taxes. To protect its sales, the industry has spent enormous amounts to oppose anti-smoking groups. These efforts, however, have not been successful even though the tobacco companies have donated millions of dollars to fight the new taxes (Ludlow). This indicates that the anti-smoking campaigns are making progress in their quest for better health and cleaner air. It's also evident that the tobacco industry will continue to fight any regulation of their product.

Paragraph 1 exemplifies poor style. The writer of this paragraph fails to integrate the source material into the text, and this produces an incoherent, choppy collection of ideas. Further, the paragraph depends too much on quoted material from one source ("Tobacco" 21–22). The quotations are neither adequately introduced nor summarized. The author's own interpretations are not presented, leaving the reader to conclude that the writer of this paragraph has not done too much thinking about the topic.

By contrast, paragraph 2 is an example of an effective style. The writer's own ideas form the frame of the paragraph; the source information is used as evidence to support the writer's views. The source material is carefully introduced and effectively woven into the text. This paragraph is easy to read because it focuses on one topic, and the connections from one sentence to the next are evident to the reader.

**Guidelines for Using Source Information**

**1.** Determine what the paragraph will focus on before you start writing. Be certain that you know how the paragraph relates to the thesis. Identify the main point you wish to stress. If you are having trouble with the focus of the paragraph, do some freewriting to discover what you want to say.

**2.** Prepare a clearly worded topic sentence, one that presents your views on the topic. Avoid using source material in the first sentence of any paragraph because this information should back up your views, not precede the introductory statement.

**3.** Select sources which are directly related to the point you wish to stress. No matter how hard you try to integrate it, irrelevant source material causes the focus of the entire paragraph to shift. If you suspect that your information doesn't support the paragraph's main point, don't use it. Do additional research to locate a more appropriate source.

**4.** Present the source material appropriately. As discussed earlier, use some type of introductory comment to integrate the information into your paragraph. Presenting the author's name and some brief identifying information is an effective introduction. (Remember that when you first mention an author give the first and last names and some brief background information. All additional references to that same author are by last name only.) Follow the source material with a sentence or two of explanation and discussion.

**5.** Do not use too many direct quotations because they often create a choppy style. Try to paraphrase some of the information even though it takes more time and effort to write a paraphrase than it does to use a quotation. Combine paraphrases and short quotations into single, complete sentences. When working with long passages, use a combination of paraphrasing and quoting. See pages 66–67 of this manual for information on this style.

**6.** When you do use direct quotations, keep them short. Avoid using the extended quotation as used in sample paragraph 1. Seldom is it necessary to use more than four lines of directly quoted material, so omit the extended quotation. If the material is important, paraphrase it.

**7.** Provide clear transitions from source material to the wording of your own ideas. Readers must be able to recognize where quotations and paraphrases begin and end, so provide clear signals. Since quotation marks are not used with a paraphrase, use other clues to indicate the beginning and ending of your source material.

**8.** Avoid long paragraphs. If your paragraph goes beyond two-thirds of a typed page, examine the content. Should the paragraph be divided into two shorter, more effective paragraphs?

**9.** End the paragraph with your own comments. Ending paragraphs with source material reveals incomplete paragraph development and careless thinking.

### Correctly Structured Paragraph

The following paragraph, taken from a paper titled "Government Funding of the Arts," demonstrates how paragraphs are structured. Remember to introduce and summarize source material with sentences presenting your opinions on the topic. Present comments and explanations to show the reader that you are thinking about the content, not just copying sections of material from sources.

Review this sample paragraph, noting that the writer's ideas serve as the frame and the source material backs up those ideas.

> The recent review of the National Endowment for the Arts (NEA) funding creates controversy. Although the Constitution guarantees freedom of expression, NEA grant recipients must meet restrictive new standards designed to guard against obscenity. According to Jim Sitter, executive director for the Council of Literary Magazines and Presses in New York, the government's official definition of "obscene" limits artistic expression, causing artists and writers to become upset and confused (Castor 2). The obvious question is, can artists produce their best work if they are hampered by narrow guidelines? Most likely the quality of their work will decline. In fact, many artists and art institutions believe that restrictions connected to government funding are "disastrous to the creative spirit of the nation" (Hentoff A21). In addition to having a negative impact on artistic expression, the NEA controversy is complicated by taxpayers' objections to the NEA's support of offensive projects. Although critics of the New NEA guidelines are fighting for the artists' freedom of expression, who is representing the indignant taxpayers? As evident the controversial issue of government funding of the arts is a problem that will not be solved easily.

This paragraph demonstrates good style because the writer attempts to involve the reader. By posing questions and addressing the concerns of typical American citizens, the writer creates a "dialogue" with the reader. The writer uses researched facts and expert opinion to substantiate the opening points. Additional comments by the author follow the source material, thus providing adequate discussion of the topic. Note that all sentences relate to the main point presented in the topic sentence, ensuring that the paragraph is unified.

Constructing effective paragraphs takes time and skill. As discussed earlier, you first must establish a clear focus: What do you want the paragraph to present? Jot down some ideas; construct an informal outline. Begin writing only after you have thought about the content. Thinking and planning—essential prewriting steps—guard against producing a jumbled mess of information.

If you like to begin your work by doing some free writing or brainstorming, remember that these prewriting steps are merely preliminary activities designed to prepare you to write your paragraphs. Don't use those paragraphs in your paper! Your freewriting must be focused and refined before you can use them. Instructors can detect final papers which consist of undeveloped, random freewriting exercises.

Once your paragraph is complete, analyze it carefully. Determine if the content is clearly and logically presented. Check to see if you effectively balanced your thoughts with the source material. Then repeat this time-consuming, yet valuable, process for the next paragraph of your paper.

CHAPTER **9**

# Revising
# Your Writing

## THE ESSENTIALS OF REVISION

Good writing demands patience, discipline, and practice. Established writers know that writing is hard work, recognizing that the product is not truly finished until it has been revised several times. Serious revision is an essential part of good writing. Students must understand that all successful writers revise their work several times because a first draft seldom produces a finished, polished paper.

Revision involves working on the draft of a paper for the purpose of achieving several goals: (1) developing the content, (2) improving the organization and unity, and (3) strengthening the wording. The revising process involves taking a careful look at what you have written and at how you have expressed your ideas. It requires more than a quick spell-check or a punctuation review; it requires you to analyze the structure and expression of your writing. Through revision you can turn an average paper into a good paper. Remember, though, that effective revision requires time and effort. This causes problems for students who believe that the paper is complete once they have produced the first draft.

## REVISING YOUR FIRST DRAFT

Once you have completed the first draft of your paper, wait a few days before you begin the process of revision. Writers note that there is a vast difference in how they respond to their work once they have moved beyond the intense stage of producing the first draft. That is, the paper presents a different impression, allowing you to get a more objective view if you can put some distance between you and your work. When you sit down to review your paper, tell yourself that you are going to make some changes in the first draft. A good strategy is to assume that your paper has some strengths but that it needs additional work before it's considered finished.

Remember that revision involves reading your work with a critical eye, looking for areas which are undeveloped or confusing. Review the basics such as the thesis statement and the supporting ideas. Look again at your audience, purpose, and tone. In addition, review the general readability and your use of sources. Consider the following questions:

**Topic:** Have I selected an interesting topic? Are my ideas on the topic well developed and thoroughly explained?

**Thesis:** Is my thesis evident throughout the paper? Does each paragraph relate to the thesis? Does the conclusion match the thesis?

**Support:** Are the supporting paragraphs well developed? Is source material presented accurately and effectively? Do the supporting paragraphs follow the lead of the thesis?

**Audience:** Who will be reading this paper? Have I explained everything my readers need to know? How will my readers respond to the ideas I am presenting?

**Tone:** Do I "talk" to my readers throughout the paper? Do I seem real or is my style artificial and inflated?

**Purpose:** What is my goal? Am I attempting to persuade the reader to accept my thesis? Is my purpose evident? Is it maintained throughout the paper?

**Readability:** Have I eliminated awkward wording? Have I used smooth transitions from one idea to the next? Does the source information have a smooth flow?

**Use of Sources:** Have I used a balanced variety of sources? Is the source material presented effectively, using the paraphrase more often than direct quotation? Are the sources documented correctly? Have I accurately listed my sources on a Works Cited list?

Most writers find that it's helpful to have someone else read a draft of their work. Select an objective, knowledgeable reader who will offer specific comments about areas that need attention. You may want to point out your concerns and ask your reader for suggestions. Remember to allow enough time for several revisions because you probably will need to revise sections of your paper several times. Students who have revised their work know that the paper improves with each version; they recognize that revision is worth the time and effort. This is a good time to use the services of a Writing Center if one is available on your campus. Writing Center tutors provide valuable assistance because they are trained to review students' work.

## A Sample of Revision

The following paragraph is taken from a student paper on the topic of gun control.

### THESIS: RESTRICTIONS ON HANDGUNS ARE NOT EFFECTIVE.

There is no way to stop criminals from getting guns. No way. They just can't be stopped. "You could probably walk into half the bars in Atlanta and walk out with an illegally purchased firearm," according to Mr. Phillips (12). Bans and restrictions on handguns will not stop criminals from getting guns or from using firearms in violent crimes. In fact, it makes the problem worse. You just can't pass laws restricting guns and expect criminals to abide by them. It's not going to happen because it doesn't make sense. In a survey of criminals, 80 percent claimed that they would use sawed off shotguns and rifles if they had no access to handguns. Restrictions on guns violate the citizens' Second Amendment right to bear arms, and this would cause problems for law abiding citizens who want to own a gun for their personal protection. When laws are passed to restrict the purchase of guns, citizens' rights are being denied.

The content of this paragraph needs some serious revision. To begin, notice that the first sentence is weak because it fails to present the main point of the paragraph and it makes no reference to the thesis statement. As you know, a weak topic sentence causes confusion, leaving the reader to wonder how the paragraph relates to the rest of the paper. Other problems with focus are also evident in this paragraph. Notice that the topic shifts. It moves away from the main point that gun control will not stop criminals from getting guns. That is a valid point, but it is not well developed. The student depends on repetition and emotional appeal rather than on solid facts to present the case. Of course, the result is a weak paragraph.

The revision of this paragraph involves making the following changes:

**1.   Focus:** Select a main point and stay with it. Eliminate information that doesn't follow that point. For example, the last two sentences reveal that the student has shifted to a new topic. Those ideas should be developed in another paragraph because they do not fit the focus of this paragraph. Introducing unrelated material reveals that serious problems exist: the student writer didn't have good source material to develop the main point or lost track of the focus. It's easy for a reader to detect this weakness because the reader recognizes that the ending sentences do not follow the opening ideas in this paragraph.

**2.   Development:** After stating your main point, develop it by presenting evidence from your sources. The source information should be used to expand and explain the main point. Avoid vague, unexplained references such as the use of "Mr. Phillips" or "a survey of criminals" because the reader has some unanswered questions: Who is he? When was the survey conducted? How many criminals were surveyed?

Remember that source material is effective only when it presents specific information that supports the point you are trying to make. Source information should answer the reader's concerns without causing the reader to question the validity of the source. Your commentary should present logical ideas based on solid reasoning, not on an emotional appeal.

Review the revised version of the same paragraph. Notice the content is stronger and the focus is easier to follow.

Gun control laws will not prevent criminals from getting guns. All criminals know that guns are readily available. According to Jed Phillips, a spokesman for the National Rifle Association, "You could probably walk into half the bars in Atlanta and walk out with an illegally purchased firearm" (12). This means that criminals will find ways to obtain weapons even though laws have been passed to regulate the sale of guns. A 1988 survey of two hundred convicted felons in New York, Chicago, and Los Angeles reveals that they would use sawed off shotguns and rifles if they had no access to handguns. They also indicated that they would use bigger and deadlier handguns if they could not find the smaller, cheap versions (Clay 1104–10). It's easy to see that criminals would improvise to get weapons, thus demonstrating that gun regulations are ineffective.

## REVISING THE WORDING OF YOUR PAPER

After you have strengthened the content of your paper through revision, it's time to review your wording. When you revise the wording of your paper you must analyze your word choice and rewrite weak areas to add strength, clarity, and directness. Do not confuse revision with proofreading—the final step of searching for mechanical errors. Completed before proofreading, revision requires an examination of word choice and sentence structure. Review the following guidelines and apply these principles to your writing.

   **1. Stress Nouns and Verbs:**   Create images for your reader through carefully chosen nouns and strong verbs. Do not plant the weight of your sentences on adjectives and adverbs. Use concrete nouns and verbs to carry the message.

   If your writing contains several "There is . . ." or "It is . . ." constructions, you are using weak, indirect wording in place of strong nouns and verbs. Note the differences between the following sentences:

Weak and Indirect    <u>It is</u> known that the virus spreads rapidly.

Strong Noun          <u>Researchers</u> know that the virus spreads rapidly.

   **2. Change Passive Voice to Active Voice:**   Passive constructions invert the normal word order, thus weakening the sentence. When possible, replace *verb phrases* (word groups tied with strings of helping verbs such as *could have been* or *is being*) with active verbs.

   The subject of your sentence performs the action when you use the active voice. In contrast, passive verbs create weak sentences because the object performs the action. This means that the construction of your sentence is turned around because the subject is receiving, not doing, the action. Passive wording makes it hard for the reader to understand your ideas.

   Analyze the sample sentences below. The first sentence depends on the awkward passive voice, while the second uses the direct active voice to make the point. Notice that the active sentences are shorter and easier to read.

Passive    Our highways <u>are being crowded</u> by heavy trucks.

Active    Heavy trucks <u>crowd</u> our highways.

Passive    <u>It is known</u> by public colleges that race-based scholarships are vulnerable to legal challenges.

Active    Public colleges <u>know</u> that race-based scholarships are vulnerable to legal challenges.

Passive    In 1996, the banning of a book <u>was challenged</u> successfully by a high school teacher in Cortland, Ohio.

Active    In 1996, a high school teacher in Cortland, Ohio, successfully <u>challenged</u> the banning of a book.

To eliminate passive voice, ask yourself a simple question: *Who is doing the action?* This will help you identify the subject of your sentence. Place the subject near the beginning of your sentence, making it easier for the reader to understand your message.

The next step is to delete unnecessary linking or helping verbs. These are forms of *to be* such as *is, are, was, were, has, have, be, been, being.* For best results, eliminate passive constructions from your writing.

**3.   Avoid Weak, Sluggish Verbs:** Uninteresting verbs (especially forms of the verb *to be*) deaden your writing because they are colorless and inexact. Change these dull words to lively, image-producing verbs. Review the example below, noting the impact of strong verbs.

Weak    Government spending <u>is</u> up every year, and the average taxpayer <u>is</u> <u>experiencing</u> the impact of this increase. They <u>are seeking relief</u>.

Improved    Since government spending <u>soars</u> yearly, increased taxes <u>punish</u> the average American. Taxpayers <u>cry</u> for tax relief.

**4.   Eliminate Unnecessary Uses of "Who" and "Which":** These words introduce dependent clauses and, in many cases, work against concise wording. The overuse of "who" and "which" loads writing with wordiness as evident in the example below. Increase reader interest through an economy of wording.

Wordy    Euthanasia, which is a controversial and complicated subject which few people feel comfortable thinking about, involves legal and moral matters which vary from one issue to the next.

Improved    Euthanasia, a controversial and complicated subject for most people, involves varying legal and moral issues.

**5.   Use Prepositional Phrases Sparingly:** These constructions often add wordiness, not precise meaning, to a sentence. Long strings of prepositional phrases fail to impress the reader. Notice the "drag" created by the prepositional phrases in this example:

Wordy      Star Wars is a collection <u>of high-tech programs of significant value</u> designed <u>by scientists</u> <u>to provide</u> <u>for the defense</u> <u>of our country</u> <u>in the event</u> <u>of a conflict</u> <u>with another country.</u>

Improved   Star Wars, a valuable collection of scientifically designed high-tech programs, provides defense against foreign aggression.

The revised version shown above attacks the eight prepositional phrases found in the original, leaving only two such constructions. The sentence flows more smoothly, presenting concise meaning to the reader.

Analyze your style. Do prepositional phrases inhibit your effectiveness? As a general guideline, it's possible to revise your wording, eliminating one-half of these weighty constructions.

**6.   Avoid Clichés:**   Some ordinary phrases lack impact because they are overused. These lax expressions reveal the writer's inability to create lively wording. Clichés are exhausted phrases that only fill space, adding little meaning to a sentence. Eliminate the following phrases from your writing:

| | |
|---|---|
| in view of the fact that | in this day and age |
| proved to be | due to the fact that |
| as far as _____ is concerned | in this land of ours today |
| too numerous to mention | in order to |
| it can be said that | and so forth |
| at this point in time | last but not least |
| wise as an owl | back on her feet |
| innocent as a lamb | rude awakening |

**7.   Avoid "In my opinion" and "I think that":**   Phrases such as "I think that," "It is my opinion that," "I feel," or "I believe" are unnecessary. They clutter your writing. The reader knows that your paper presents your views, so it's not necessary to label the information as your opinion.

When expressing someone else's view or presenting information from a source, use appropriate wording so the reader knows that those opinions are not yours. Wording such as "Dr. Mack describes" or "The author notes" helps the reader understand who is the source of the information.

Another important note—it's OK to use "I" in your research writing. Many students experience confusion about the voice to use when writing a college paper, believing that they should "never use I." They are misled by this advice. For some college research papers, using the first person pronoun is acceptable. Problems develop, however, when "I" is overused to the point that one sentence after the next begins with "I think that" or "I feel." Discuss this issue with your instructor.

Remember some of the basics of writing: As the author, you are talking to your reader, attempting to establish common ground so as to advance your position. If your style is stiff and removed (i.e., "This researcher believes that . . ."), your persona as a writer is less credible. You will seem detached from your topic and from your reader's concerns.

Be sensible about your writing. Use "I" when necessary. For example, if you are describing a survey that you conducted, you will have to use wording that includes the personal pronoun "I." Notice the difference in the styles of these samples:

Poor   To investigate the problem of poor health care, this researcher surveyed thirty-four patients at the Bakerstown Health Clinic.

Better   To investigate the problem of poor health care, I surveyed thirty-four patients at the Bakerstown Health Clinic.

**8.   Avoid Pompous, Elaborate Wording:**   Making a simple statement complicated by using more words and longer words causes problems for the reader. Although some student writers believe that an elaborate style is scholarly and sophisticated, readers are not impressed. Effective wording is direct and lively, not embellished with ornate language as shown in this example:

On the auspicious occasion of your natal day, I extend felicitations.
(In simple terms, Happy Birthday to you!)

The best advice is to write brief, sensible sentences. Use words from the thesaurus sparingly and intelligently. When student writers use a thesaurus to locate synonyms, often they make the mistake of using (and misusing) unfamiliar words because they sound impressive. Avoid the temptation to impress your readers.

**9.   Eliminate Vague Wording:**   Vague words add little substance to a sentence because they are too general. Replacing exhausted words with concrete, direct language builds reader interest. Avoid these meaningless words:

| | | | |
|---|---|---|---|
| a lot of | many | numerous | several |
| aspect | different | much | people |
| thing | phase | interesting | nice |
| seem | pretty good | | |

Review the following sentence. What does it mean? Does the vague, indirect wording hide the meaning?

Vague   The many different factors that are involved in government spending seem to be causing a lot of problems for people.

Improved   Government spending causes taxpayer problems.

Improved   Taxpayers suffer when the government overspends.

In both of the improved versions above, precise language creates a more direct sentence. As you can see, revision produces better wording.

**10.   Use Precise Wording:**   Select words carefully. Don't settle for the first words that come to mind because these choices are often close, yet not exact. Analyze your sentences; think about the meaning and the word choice. Remember that inaccurate *diction* (word choice) confuses the reader. Note the faulty wording in the following examples:

> Brainy students study constantly. In fact the high grades of these workhorses <u>verify</u> the time they spend on their studies. (justify?)

> For females suffering from anorexia, the heart cannot function at a normal, healthy <u>perspective</u>. (rate?)

> The smart driver uses seatbelts to avoid <u>accidents</u>. (injuries?)

> For students eating in the cafeteria, the <u>remote</u> serving times cause problems. (limited?)

Serious problems with diction cause these sentences to "fall apart" for the reader. Avoid errors in diction by reviewing your wording carefully.

**Sample Revision of Wording**

Review the following sample paragraphs. Note that the revised paragraph is easier to read because the wording is direct and concise.

**Original Paragraph**

*Use active voice*

*Web users must understand that the*

~~There are a lot of really good reasons why only a limited~~ amount of material is available
                                                    *is limited.*
on the World Wide Web. ~~I think that students and other people who use the Web should~~

~~understand that the practical matter involves one very important issue—money.~~ According-

ing to William Miller, president of the Association of College and Research Libraries,
                                                                                *will not*
publishers of ~~books and articles used by students for college~~ research ~~are not inclined to~~
                                    *electronically*                                        *Eliminat*
make materials available ~~in an electronic format~~ because they must "protect their current   *wordines*
                        *Presently, digitizing a book is*
profit margins" (A44). ~~At this point in time, it is an extremely~~ expensive. ~~operation to digi-~~

*Omit the obvious*

~~tize an entire book just to have it made available to Web users. In my opinion, it is evi-~~
                *p*                *current*                                *know that they cannot*
~~dent that the~~ publishers of books ~~which are currently on the market will not~~ make a profit

if they make their copyrighted materials available on the Web at no cost. ~~to the user of~~

~~the information.~~

**Revised Paragraph**

Web users must understand that the amount of material available on the World Wide Web is limited due to financial concerns. According to William Miller, president of the Association of College and Research Libraries, publishers will not make materials available electronically because they must "protect their current profit margins" (A44). Presently, digitizing a book is expensive. Publishers of current materials know that they cannot make a profit if they make their copyrighted materials available on the Web at no cost.

## GUIDELINES FOR EFFICIENT PROOFREADING

**1.** Plan to proofread your paper. Make proofreading a regular step in your composition process. Set aside time when you can devote total concentration and sufficient time to the task.

**2.** Do not proof your work immediately after you finish composing it. Your effectiveness diminishes if you do not allow some time to elapse before rereading your material.

**3.** Avoid proofing your paper on the computer screen. For best results, print out a copy of your work. Attempt to evaluate your writing with an objective, critical eye.

**4.** Focus individual attention on every line and on every word. Proceed slowly enough so you can see what is actually on the paper, not what you had intended to put there. Pointing to each word might reduce your speed, but it will increase your accuracy.

**5.** Read your paper aloud to yourself and/or to another person. This process refines all elements of the composition from coherence, tone, and mechanics to overall effectiveness. Oral reading improves the accuracy of your proofing. Try it.

**6.** Proofread with a pencil or pen in your hand, so you can mark or correct the errors as you find them. If you are making corrections on the final copy, use black ink or a sharp pencil.

**7.** Always have a dictionary and a grammar book handy. Use these resources if there is the slightest doubt of accuracy. Take the time to look it up or consult someone who might know.

**8.** Use the spell-check program on the word processor, but remember that a computer program cannot differentiate between the correct and the incorrect use of a word. Since these programs only locate spelling errors, you must check for accurate usage.

**9.** Ask a reliable friend to read your paper. An objective reader may uncover problems you failed to notice. Even though you may consult with another person, remember that you are responsible for the content and form of your own paper.

**10.** Check the general appearance of your paper before deciding if it is ready to be turned in. Look for neat, legible corrections.

## FORMAT OF A RESEARCH PAPER

When preparing the final copy of your research paper, use a standard format. If your instructor does not specify a style, follow the guidelines presented here.

### Ink Cartridge and Paper

Use standard white 8-$\frac{1}{2}$ × 11 paper. Be certain that the ink cartridge or the ribbon in your printer or typewriter is fresh enough to produce an easily readable copy. If the type is light, change the ribbon or get a new ink cartridge.

### The Title of Your Paper

Always give your paper a title, remembering that the title should not be a complete sentence. Do not underline it or put it in quotation marks. Further, do not type the title in all capital letters. Review these guidelines for capitalization of words in a title:

- Capitalize all major words in the title.
- Capitalize the first word and the last word in the title.
- Capitalize an article ("A," "An," or "The") only when it is the first word of the title.
- Do not capitalize short prepositions (of, on, to, in) when they are in the title. However, capitalize prepositions of five letters or more (above, about, throughout, without, against).
- Do not capitalize coordinating conjunctions (and, but, or) when used within a title. However, other conjunctions (when, although, while) should be capitalized. Note these examples:
    Insurance Problems for Our Cities
    The Duties of a Congressional Representative
- When using a subtitle, use a colon and capitalize the first word after the colon as shown in this example:
    Man Against Nature: Who Wins?
- Do not place a period after the title.

**Margins**

All margins (top, bottom, right, and left) should be one inch. If you are using a title page, the following spacing should be used for the first page of your paper:

---

Line 7                                    Center Title Here

Line 14        Begin your paper here. Remember not to underline the title of your paper.

**Spacing**

Always double-space a paper. In addition, use double-spacing for extended quotations. All entries in the Works Cited should be double-spaced, with double-spacing between entries as well. Use hanging indentation for Works Cited entries. That is, type the first line flush with the left margin while indenting five spaces for all other lines in each entry. (See pages 112–13 for additional information on preparing the Works Cited list.)

**Page Numbers**

Number all pages after the first page, including the Works Cited page. Present your last name and the page number in the upper right-hand corner, one-half inch from the top (on line four). No punctuation goes between your name and the page number. Omit "p." or "page." Space one-half inch (four lines) below the name and page number before typing the paper. The first line of your paper should begin on line seven.

**Title Page**

Although the MLA Handbook for Writers of Research Papers states that a title page is unnecessary, you may wish to use one for your paper. The traditional title page consists of the paper's title, author's name, information about the course, and the date.

Double-space and center all items. Refer to the sample papers (pages 120–39) in this manual for examples of title pages.

If you prefer not to use a title page, present the heading (your name, instructor's name, class, and date) flush with the left margin, one inch from the top of the first page. Leave a space between these items. Leave two lines between the heading and title, and then center your title. Allow four blank lines before typing the text. The following sample presents this format:

**First Page with Heading**

---

*Line 7* ⟶ Bonnie McDonald
AH 408.08
Prof. Zevin
May 13, 1998

⎫
⎬ *Double space*
⎭

Studying Art History in Italy

⎫
⎬ *Four blank lines*
⎭

Begin your paper here. You should allow four blank lines after the title.

---

**Works Cited**

Alphabetize entries according to the author's last name. If no author is given, use the first word in the title other than "A," "An," or "The."

An alphabetical listing is important because this arrangement allows the reader to locate the complete publication information for a source cited in your paper. Guidelines for preparing the Works Cited are as follows:

**1.**   All sources cited in the paper must be listed in the Works Cited.

**2.**   The Works Cited should not include sources that are not used in the paper. If you used sources for preliminary reading but did not cite them in the paper, these sources *should not* appear in the Works Cited. You may wish to prepare a separate list, called Works Consulted, for these sources.

**3.**    The citations in the paper must be keyed to the Works Cited list.

When typing the Works Cited page, follow the format shown below. Center the title Works Cited on the seventh line of the page. Do not underline or use quotation marks around the title Works Cited. Double-space after this title and begin listing sources. Type the first line of each entry flush with the left margin, but indent five spaces for successive lines within the entry. Return to the left margin for the next entry. Double-space each entry and double-space between each entry.

Line 4                                                                                        Goodson 12

                                                                                     Your Name   Page

Line 7                                           Works Cited

Natale, Jo Anna. "High-tech and Social Isolation: On-line School for Home Learners."

        Education Digest 61 (1995): 36+.

Shea, Christopher. "From Home to College: Admissions Officers Grapple with How to

        Evaluate Applicants Educated Outside School." Chronicle of Higher Education 42

        (1996): A31.

Zirkel, Perry A. "Home Sweet School." Phi Delta Kappan 76 (1994): 332–34.

**Annotated Bibliography**

Begin with a complete bibliography in MLA style. Present a *brief* summary (two or three sentences) of the source. Use appropriate wording in the summary. That is, refer to the author and use present tense verbs.

Present the items in your annotated bibliography in alphabetical order. Single-space the bibliographic information and double-space the summary. Check your work for conciseness and accuracy. Note the following examples:

**Annotated Bibliography**

Evered, David and Philippe Lazar. "Misconduct in Medical Research." <u>Lancet</u> 345 (1995): 1161–63.

Evered and Lazar explore ethical issues in medical research and identify ways to avoid misconduct. They suggest that continued emphasis on high standards, as demonstrated by senior researchers who should serve as role models for students, is essential.

Burd, Stephen. "Research Powerhouse Under the Microscope." <u>Chronicle of Higher Education</u> 40 (1994): A24+.

Burd discusses the case of scientific misconduct that was investigated by the University of Pittsburgh. He notes that the biased investigation suggests that the institution was trying to hide the misconduct because they didn't want to lose federal research grants.

Horvitz, Leslie Alan. "Can Scientists Police Themselves?" <u>Insight</u> 10 (1994): 6+.

Horvitz focuses on the lack of professional ethics among scientific researchers and raises questions about scientists' ability to monitor their own work. He discusses the work of the Office of Research Integrity and concludes that this organization has been ineffective in managing misconduct cases.

# CHAPTER **10**

# Mechanics in Writing with Sources

## BRACKETS

Use brackets to show that you added or changed material in a direct quotation. You may add an explanation or clarification; however, do not make changes in the original unless you use brackets to indicate your modification. Note the examples below:

> According to a recent <u>National Review</u> article, "The Parents; Rights and Responsibilities Act is their [parents'] way of waging a war against school systems that teach inappropriate sexual education classes" (55).

> Lloyd writes, "Of all composers, he [Franz Peter Stubbier] has been called the last of the classical composers and the first of the Romantics" (512).

## CAPITALIZATION IN QUOTED MATERIAL

Although quoted material generally is reproduced exactly as it appears in the original, you may change the initial capitalization to make the quotation blend grammatically into the sentence. Review the following guidelines, noting that *brackets are not used to indicate a capitalization change.*

**Original**

If a simple blood test could identify these markers and predict the children who might develop heart disease later in life, preventive measures—such as low-fat, low-cholesterol diets and stepped-up exercise—could begin early.

**1.**   Use a capital letter if the quotation is a complete sentence. When the quotation is not a complete sentence, use a lower case letter. In the sample below, note the capitalization change in "preventive."

> Scientists at California Biotechnology, Inc. discovered chemical "markers" in the DNA of white blood cells used to indicate those predisposed to heart disease. Clark, Hager, and Stadtman write, "Preventive measures—such as low-fat, low-cholesterol diets and stepped-up exercise—could begin early" (23).

**2.**   When the word *that* precedes the quotation, use a lower case letter and omit the comma.

> Researchers report that "forty percent of 157 test subjects who had signs of heart disease exhibited abnormalities in genes involved in transporting cholesterol and fats in the blood." (Clark, Hager, and Stadtman 23).

## COLON

To introduce a long quotation with a grammatically complete sentence, use a colon. The example below shows this style:

> Schindler's article in <u>American History Illustrated</u> describes the circumstances leading to the bombing of Chicago's Haymarket Square: "A group of radicals had taken over much of the labor and union leadership, especially among the German immigrant workers, who had seen other immigrant groups as strikebreakers" (21).

Remember not to use the colon after a linking verb or after a preposition. When quoting passages of more than four typed lines, use the extended quotation format. See the section titled "Extended Quotation," pages 118–19, for information on this style.

## CONTENT ENDNOTES OR EXPLANATORY NOTES

On occasion you may need a *content endnote* in your paper. These notes, also called *explanatory notes*, are brief additions of information essential to the content of your paper. Their use should be limited to (1) supplementary material or explanations that cannot be incorporated into the text or (2) bibliographic information.

The following example shows a content note and the use of a superscript numeral in the text. According to the MLA style, endnotes appear on a separate sheet after the text. This new page is numbered in sequence and the title "Notes" is centered 1 inch from the top. All information is double-spaced, with the first line of each note indented five spaces, as shown in the following example:

> Special provisions must be made to accommodate the needs of the elderly who wish to join the work force. According to Michaels (50), a 1996 Harris Poll indicates that most older workers prefer part-time work. The limited schedule provides the economic and psychological benefits essential for many elderly.

### Notes

> According to the Harris Poll, the reasons for this preference are not evident. For detailed information, see <u>Journal of Social Issues and Sociological Review</u>.

Avoid overusing endnotes. In most cases, you should be able to include the information in your text, so endnotes will be unnecessary.

## ELLIPSIS

To show that you have omitted part of a quoted passage, use ellipsis (three spaced periods). This mark indicates that your quotation is not an exact reproduction of the original. Do not use ellipsis when quoting only a word or a phrase. In this case the deletion will be obvious to your reader, so the ellipsis mark is unnecessary.

The ellipsis mark allows you to omit unessential information from a passage, thus reducing the amount of quoted material. Note that the remaining sentence parts must form grammatically complete sentences when the omissions have been made. The following examples are based on "In Defense of Government Regulation" by Price and Simowitz in *Journal of Economic Issues.*

### Original

> A first step in defense of the legitimacy of government regulation is to increase public awareness of an alternate, more explicitly political view of property rights. This alternative view stresses the fact that property is inevitably a social, legal, and political institution. Many Americans think of property as physical entities such as land, houses, and cars. A smaller number of people would also include more intangible items such as inventions, creative ideas, or a company's trade name. The political perspective, however, stresses that it is not the intrinsic qualities of these items that define them as property.

**1.   Middle-of-a-Sentence Deletion:**   Use the ellipsis mark to indicate where unessential information has been deleted. Remember to form a grammatically complete sentence with the remaining sentence parts.

> When arguing for the government's right to regulation, Price and Simowitz emphasize that "a first step . . . is to increase public awareness of an alternate, more explicitly political view of property rights" (168).

**2.  End of Sentence Deletion:**   Use the ellipsis mark and then end the sentence with a period after the parenthetical reference as shown below:

> Price and Simowitz note that many Americans want to "increase public awareness of an alternate, more explicitly political view . . . (168)."

**3.  Complete Sentence Deletion:**   End the preceding sentence with a period. Space once and use the ellipsis mark. As indicated below, the result is four periods for a complete sentence deletion. (One period ends the "Many Americans" sentence, and the other three periods are the ellipsis mark.) In the following example, a complete sentence was omitted from the original.

> Some experts question the meaning of property: "Many Americans think of property as physical entities such as land, houses, and cars. . . . The political perspective, however, stresses that it is not the intrinsic qualities of these items that define them as property" (Price and Simowitz 168).

## EXTENDED QUOTATION

When quoting lengthy passages, use the format for an extended quotation. According to the MLA handbook, directly quoted material of more than four typed lines should be indented ten spaces and double-spaced. Do not adjust the right margin when "blocking" a quotation.

If the sentence preceding the extended quotation is a grammatically complete sentence, use a colon to introduce the quotation. Do not indent the first line if the extended quotation is a single paragraph or less.

The following example shows the correct format for an extended quotation. Note that quotation marks are not used. However, use double (not single) quotation marks in a blocked quotation if the original contains quotation marks.

> The issue of sexual discrimination in collegiate athletic programs deserves attention. The results of a 1996 survey reveal that female athletes are not given the same opportunities as their male counterparts. In a recent <u>Chronicle of Higher Education</u> article, Lederman discusses this inequity:   Use Colon Here
>> Men's teams receive almost 70 percent of the athletic scholarship money, 77 percent of the operating money, and 83 percent of the recruiting money spent by colleges that play big-time sports, according to a recent study on sex equity by the National Collegiate Athletic Association. Advocates for women's sports said the study shows clearly that the average Division I college was in violation of Title IX of the Education Amendments of 1972, the laws that bar sex discrimination at institutions that receive federal aid. (A1)
>
> Period Before Citation

Note that the final period goes *before* the citation when using the block quotation. Limit your use of extended quotations. Use this style only if a lengthy section from a source is essential to your paper. Do not use several extended quotations within one paper because readers are distracted by long blocks of quoted material. Avoid using extended quotations by paraphrasing some of the material and by quoting the remainder.

## *SIC*

If the section you wish to quote contains an error, insert *sic* (a Latin word meaning "thus" or "so") in square brackets. [Write the brackets by hand if your word processor or typewriter does not have these characters.] This insertion indicates that the error was in the original and is not your mistake. The use of *sic* in the example below reveals that the misspelling of megadoses occurred in the original.

> According to Stoetzel, "Water-soluble vitamins are not entirely safe if taken in megdoses [sic]" (78).

## SINGLE QUOTATION MARKS

A "quotation within a quotation" occurs when your source contains a quotation. Use single quotation marks within the regular double quotation marks to indicate that a quotation appeared in the original. Review the following examples:

> Katel discusses the problem of overcrowded prisons and notes that "prosecutors say they have no choice but to resort increasingly to the 'habitual criminal' law, specifying that 'habituals' must serve at least 70 percent of their sentences before they become eligible for release" (63).

> According to the authors of <u>The Unsinkable Titanic</u>, "The ship appeared 'like an enormous glowworm' at sea" (28).

For additional information on using a source which contains a direct quotation, see "Using Indirect (Secondary) Sources," pages 24–25 and 71–72.

CHAPTER **11**

Sample
Student
Papers

*One inch*

Stephanie Goodermuth

Professor Missildine

English Composition II

8 May 199_

}  *Double-space*

*No quotation marks or underlining for title*  ( Time for Change: The Need for Year-Round School

|  *Double-space*

**1**   America has long been a country that thrives on competition with other

*Indent 1/2"*

countries. This competition ranges from the arms race to athletics. Why don't we

apply this competitive nature to our educational system? The answer, plain and

simple, is that Americans are stuck in an educational rut. Now as we move into the

twenty-first century, the United States lags behind many countries in educational

achievement, even behind some Third World countries. Educators recognize that

schools suffer from a variety of problems, from overcrowded classrooms and un-

motivated students to inadequate materials. The problem of poor academic

progress, however, has an obvious solution. To improve education in the United

**10**   States, the school year must be extended beyond the traditional 180 days. A year-

round school calendar has many advantages.

To begin, consider the history of American schooling. The school calendar

has always been lenient, allowing children to stay home to help their families har-

vest crops during the summer months. According to "the Case for More School

Days," attendance was not required during most of the last century, so students

were free to attend when they were available. The first attendance requirement was

enacted in 1852 in Massachusetts, calling for a minimum of twelve weeks of

*One inch*  (left)

*One inch*  (right)

*General in-formation as topic narrows and focuses on thesis*

*Thesis statement*

*History of the problem and background information*

*One inch*

Goodermuth 2

**1** schooling (Barrett 89). This system was appropriate for the early days of public edu-

cation and in times when young people could make a living without adequate

schooling. In the latter part of the nineteenth century, though, a 180-day calendar

became commonplace, accommodating the rural harvest schedule (Warrick-Harris

283). Times have changed, yet the agriculturally sensitive calendar remains. Educa-

tors know that school districts legally are able to extend the school year, but they

choose to follow the minimum standards (Forbes 25). Although the limited 180-day

school year served the agricultural society of the past, this outdated calendar must

change to accommodate year-round schooling.

**10**          Now is the time for an extended school year because Americans are begin-

ning to accept the fact that something must be done about our schools. A 1996 poll

reveals that the public approval rate of a year-round plan has increased 100 percent          *Statistics*

during the past thirty years, with 61 percent of the respondents indicating that they

support a longer school year (VanderHooven 311). These numbers clearly indicate

growing support. Americans are learning that year-round schooling is typical in many

other countries. Most European students attend well over 200 days a year. In fact,          *Comparison*

the United States has one of the shortest school years, falling behind countries such

as Israel with 216 days, Thailand with 200 days, and Hungary with 192 days. Further,

Japan demands the most of its students with 243 days a year ("Longer"). As a result          *— Citation for*
*article with no*
*author given.*
**20** of fewer instructional days, American students' test scores in math, reading compre-          *Use shortened*
*title. See pages*
hension science, and language fall below the scores of students from other coun-          *73–74.*

tries. Teachers and administrators agree that this lack of academic achievement re-

lates to the short school year. To better understand this situation, I talked with Dr.

Goodermuth 3

**1**   June Sidle of the Cleveland Area Public Schools. She claims that American students
are being denied a full education because of the 180-day calendar. She notes that
other countries will continue to have educational advantages because American parents and educators "fail to understand the importance of year-round schooling."
Even though support is growing for a change in the traditional school calendar,
some problems are evident.

*Personal interview to obtain expert opinion. No citation needed but inter-view is included in Works Cited. See pages 75–76.*

Much opposition exists to extending the school year, and the criticism is not
without merit. The most valid objection is the cost. Opponents claim that the cost of
salaries and extra materials would increase our taxes (Forbes 25). Without a doubt,

**10**   increasing instructional time has tremendous impact on the school budget, and citizens who support a new school calendar are aware of this idea. According to budget specialists, however, it is possible to alleviate financial concerns through federal

*Citation for three or more authors. See pages 75–76.*

grants and through special funding from corporate donations (Cash et al. 232–41).
Financial concerns are not the only objection. Another criticism of the longer school
year comes from parents who are concerned about the loss of the traditional summer vacation. Of course, this is a time for relaxation and fun, but one point to remember is that the extended school year does not eliminate the entire summer vacation. It simply shortens it to one month. Many critics fail to realize that many
parents support the shorter vacation, especially those who depend on day care for

**20**   elementary school children during the summer months (Daniels 33). A third concern
is that students are exhausted from the 180-day school year and that a longer year
would cause stress and create a lack of interest in learning. This is a valid issue, and
educators are very aware of this problem, but this concern is being addressed by

*Counter argument*

*Objection #1
State objections of critics*

*Refutation
Argue against critics' point*

*Objection #2*

*Refutation*

*Objection #3
Make a concession, acknowledging that critics have a valid concern. A concession increases the writer's credibility.*

Goodermuth 4

**1**

using a less intense curriculum during the warm summer months. An example of this

can be seen in the successful year-round program in El Paso County, New Mexico, a

program that fills its curriculum with high-interest enrichment activities that involve

active student participation (Barber 33). This indicates that practical solutions can

make year-round school a reality. Of course, the objections to the new calendar

should be recognized, but the benefits that are realized by an extended year out-

weigh the negative aspects.

*Refutation*

*Restatement of thesis*

　　　　The major reason for extending the school year is to strengthen students'

academic performance. Dr. Chontos, Director of Educational Policy and Planning,

**10**

describes the positive impact of year-round schooling in his article titled "Year-round

Schooling: An Evaluative Report of Six Southwestern States." He studied the

achievement test scores of 4,500 students in the areas of reading comprehension

and mathematics and concludes that students in the traditional program did not

score as well because they did not receive an adequate number of hours of class-

room instruction. Students who did participate in year-round schooling, by contrast,

achieved scores that showed the growth of eighteen to twenty months (qtd. in

Haenn 2). These numbers indicate that year-round schooling produces good results.

Hundreds of school districts throughout the United States have experimented with a

year-round calendar, and the results are impressive. For example, consider the

**20**

progress of Balfour Elementary School students in Asheboro, North Carolina. Their

test scores improved by 39 percent after two years of an extended school calendar

as compared to a similar group of students who were on the traditional system (War-

lock-Harris 289). Other studies provide additional support for year-round schooling.

*Reason #1 Part A*

*Expert opinion*

*Statistics*

*Using indirect (secondary) source. See pages 24–25 and 71–72.*

*Statistics*

Goodermuth 5

**1**    The majority of schools on the year-round system claim higher test scores as well as

improved attendance and student motivation (Bradford). These positive results can

be seen in other districts as well. In fact, no school has experienced a decline in

achievement because of the extended year, a significant point considering that the

test scores of inner-city students often fluctuate from one year to the next (Kneese

61). Academic progress is possible when students spend enough time in the class-

room, giving them the opportunity to complete the necessary materials before mov-

ing to the next grade. Teachers note that the traditional system does not allow them

to finish a textbook or to complete the required topics ("Needed" 4). As evident, stu-

**10**    dents will have a greater chance to experience academic success through year-

round schooling.

When instructional time increases, more in-depth learning takes place. The

result is better education. Teachers in Japan, for example, have a more relaxed pace

and don't feel the need to rush through lessons because they spend more days in

the classroom ("Longer School"). These teachers may work for an entire class period

on one or two math problems, a pace unknown in American schools because of the

limited number of instructional days. Without a doubt, this is one of the reasons that

Japanese students ranked second out of fifteen countries when tested on advanced

algebra, calculus, and geometry (Cash et al. 233). A reasonable assumption is that

**20**    the math skills of American students would improve if teachers devoted more time

to detailed explanations and in-depth problem solving.

In addition to improved academic performance, year-round schooling pro-

motes enthusiasm among teachers and students. Teachers feel less stress, and this

*Citation for lecture or presentation*

*Restate reason to emphasize main point of this paragraph*

*Reason #1 Part B Comparison*

*Transitional topic sentence adds coherence*

*Reason #2*

Goodermuth 6

**1**  is reflected in their positive attitudes. Educational researchers describe the increased

job satisfaction teachers experience when a longer school year allows for more in-

structional time. They note that teachers feel "more motivated to explore students'

individual learning styles" because the pace allows for greater flexibility with the cur-

riculum (Barrett 79). Of course, the learning environment improves as teachers expe-

rience greater satisfaction in the classroom, and this is definitely a positive endorse-    *Conclusions about teachers' attitudes*

ment of year-round schooling. As we readily recognize, enthusiastic teaching creates

greater interest in learning.

*Transitional*          Another advantage of year-round schooling is the availability of more time to    *Reason #3*

**10**  *topic*   study a wider variety of subjects. With an extended school year, more time could be
*sentence*

given to subjects such as art, music, and foreign language—areas that receive little

or no attention in the present system. Teachers would also have more time for en-

richment activities and for learning that goes beyond the classroom. Field trips,

workshops, and special projects are just some examples. Teachers could experi-

ment with innovative teaching methods such as team teaching and collaborative

learning (Barber 35). These new approaches increase enthusiasm and productivity.

Isn't this what American schools need? Other benefits of a longer school year, ac-

cording to a paper presented by Dr. Joseph F. Haenn at the meeting of the American    *Expert opinion*

Educational Research Association, include a better system for delivering student

**20**  support services. He notes that instructional planning at the school level was im-

proved because year-round school created a need to coordinate remediation and

assessment services (2–3). This means that students benefit from more efficient,    *Explanation of source information*

more effective support programs. Certainly taxpayers would agree with this ap-

Goodermuth 7

1       proach because they are getting more for their tax dollars.

A final advantage of year-round schooling is that it eliminates the traditional            *Reason #4*

three-month summer vacation. As it is now, weeks and even months of each new

school year are spent reviewing last year's work before starting new material. Educa-

tors estimate that students lose a significant amount of the content from the previ-

ous year (Daniels 32). Students fail to retain the material because of the three-month

gap in their education, so time-consuming reviews become necessary. The above-                *Common
knowledge doesn't
need citation. See
pages 58–59.*

average students who know the material do not benefit from extensive review; these

students become bored and their interest in learning decreases as teachers devote

10      valuable class time to teaching lessons that were covered last year. In fact, educa-

tors believe that the endless review time could be better spent by all students

(Kneese 68–70). The information that is lost during the lengthy summer vacation can

be vital to understanding important concepts. Consider the bilingual children who

must live for three months with families and in neighborhoods where English is not

spoken (Tawasha 22). Undoubtedly, this separation from the English language is

detrimental for students who are learning a new language in school. With the sum-

mer vacation shortened to one month, the retention of information is likely to im-

prove.

*Topic sentence focuses on
thesis reminding readers
of main*       20      inating the long summer vacation may help keep students out of trouble both in and
*point of paper*

Along with academic gains, year-round schooling brings social benefits. Elim-       *Reason #5*

out of school. Because a year-round program often eases school overcrowding by

using staggered schedules, there are fewer discipline problems and the school atmo-

sphere is more conducive to learning (Venable 25). In addition, teachers have more

Goodermuth 8

time to deal with discipline problems when they do occur. Another point is that the

longer school year reduces the amount of time children are exposed to the dangers

of drugs and violence that they often witness on the streets. Sociologists believe

that schools "protect vulnerable children from the negative elements" of inner-city

life (Tawasha 21). Critics of the extended calendar must acknowledge that schools          *Recognition of opposition's concerns*

are responsible for more than just education. For example, schools provide regular

meals for thousands of low-income children and are the source of essential drug

and sex education. Should young people be denied these vital services for three

long months because educators continue to follow a traditional school calendar that

is over one hundred years old? Recognizing the function of today's schools is es-

sential to improving the overall quality of education.

　　Numerous other reforms are needed in the American educational system, but          *Conclusion*

the move to year-round schooling is one of the most important. Americans pride

themselves on being competitive and hard working. Our expectations cannot be-

come reality, however, if we continue with an outdated educational system. As          *Review ideas from introduction and from body of paper*

Americans continue to fall further behind other countries, we wonder if we will be

able to meet the technological and scientific complexities of the next century. Will

we be able to maintain a competitive position if we are not preparing our young peo-

ple to meet tomorrow's challenges? Can we ignore the weaknesses of our educa-

tional system when we are dealing with the futures of our children and of our coun-

try? Yes, we can. That is why we must work for higher standards. Increasing the          *Restate thesis*

length of the school year is a good place to start.

*One half inch*

Goodermuth 9

Works Cited

*Double-space*

**1**  Barber, R. Jerry. "Year-round Schooling Really Works." <u>Education Digest</u> 62.2 (1996):

*Indent*
*1/2"*    →    31–34.

*Double-space*
*entire Works*
*Cited page*

Barrett, Michael J. "The Case for More School Days." <u>Atlantic Monthly</u> Nov. 1996:

78+.

Bradford, James C., Jr. "Year-round Schools: A Twenty year Follow-Up Study of a

*Entry for*
*lecture or*          Nationally Recognized Single Track Four-Quarter Plan at the High School
*presentation*

Level." Annual Meeting of the American Educational Research Association.

New York. 12 Apr. 1996.

Cash, Robin et al. "Reinventing Community by Changing the Academic Calendar:

**10**          Changing Time and the Consequences." <u>Year-round Education: A Collection</u>

<u>of Articles</u>. Ed. Robin Forage. Arlington Heights, IL: Skylight. 1996. 232–41.

Daniels, Alex. "Schools That (Almost) Never Close." <u>Governing</u> 8.9 (1995) 32+.   ←   *Use + to indicate*
*noncontinuous*
*pages*

Forbes, Steve. "Quality Time." <u>Forbes</u> 154.6 (1994) 25–27.

Haenn, Joseph F. "Evaluating the Promise of Single-Track Year-round Schools." An-

nual Meeting of the American Educational Research Association. New York. 9

Apr. 1996. Online U of Detroit Lib. Internet. 1 Jan. 1997. Available.

*Entry for online*
*source. Give date*
*when you consulted*
*electronic source*

Kneese, Carolyn Calvin. "Review of Research on Student Learning in Year- round

Education." <u>Journal of Research and Development in Education</u> 29.2 (1996)

*No author given*         60–72.

**20**       "Longer School Year Ahead?" <u>USA Today</u> Aug. 1990: 11.

"Needed: A Longer School Year?" <u>Current Events</u> 96:17 (1997) 3–4.

*One inch*   →   Sidel, June. Personal Interview. 7 Mar. 1997.

*One inch*

*One inch*

*One inch*

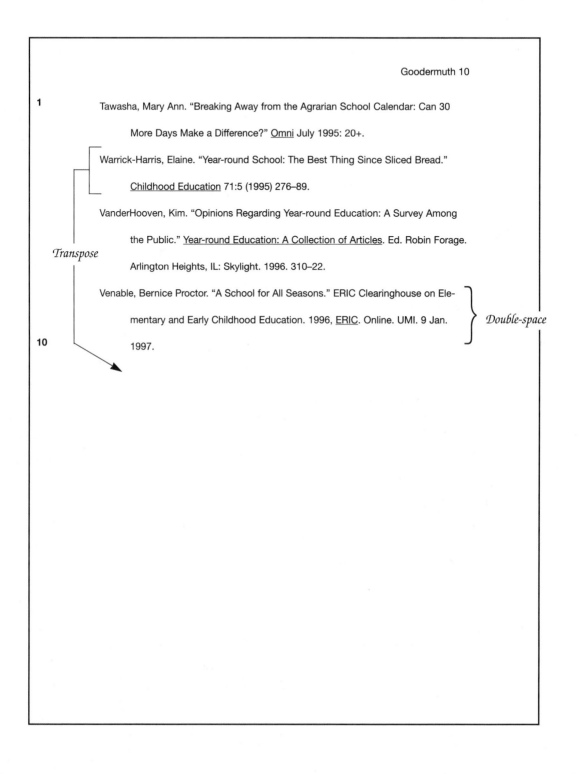

Goodermuth 10

**1**

Tawasha, Mary Ann. "Breaking Away from the Agrarian School Calendar: Can 30

More Days Make a Difference?" <u>Omni</u> July 1995: 20+.

Warrick-Harris, Elaine. "Year-round School: The Best Thing Since Sliced Bread."

<u>Childhood Education</u> 71:5 (1995) 276–89.

VanderHooven, Kim. "Opinions Regarding Year-round Education: A Survey Among

the Public." <u>Year-round Education: A Collection of Articles</u>. Ed. Robin Forage.

*Transpose*

Arlington Heights, IL: Skylight. 1996. 310–22.

Venable, Bernice Proctor. "A School for All Seasons." ERIC Clearinghouse on Ele-

mentary and Early Childhood Education. 1996, <u>ERIC</u>. Online. UMI. 9 Jan.            *Double-space*

**10**

1997.

Benson 1

Robert Benson

Professor Joseph

Freshman Composition I

9 Dec. 1997

The Threat of Affirmative Action

**1**       African Americans have been the victims of injustice for years. After slavery

ended, blacks continued to suffer from discrimination. According to Dr. Thomas

Nagel, professor of philosophy at New York University, our society was one of segre-

gation and prejudice (181). The Civil Rights laws outlawed discrimination, but there

was a need to guarantee that blacks would receive equal opportunities. The result

was the implementation of an affirmative action policy. Although the original inten-

tion was to give minorities better chances to succeed, affirmative action programs

led to the preferential treatment of minorities—even if their credentials were weak

(Schrag 11). This policy initiated quotas which required businesses to hire a set

**10**      number of minorities and to establish a system of set-asides which provided oppor-

tunities for those who could not qualify for employment. The provisions also applied

to college admissions. Even though the original affirmative action guidelines were

based on good intentions, they have evolved into a policy that promotes discrimina-

tion. <u>Affirmative action policies have a negative impact on society</u>.

      The most evident argument against affirmative action is that it is unfair. Since

the enactment of affirmative action programs, employers have been required to con-

sider minorities foremost in the employment process, even to the exclusion of more

*Expert opinion*

*Background
information.
Explain
affirmative
action*

*Thesis
statement*

*No page number in
citation for one-
page article*

**1**    qualified applicants (Nelton). What does this mean for American businesses? This

policy forces them to adopt a system of discrimination against nonminorities, a

practice contrary to the ideal of equal opportunity upon which this country was

founded. Consider the case of a white teacher who was laid off from her job with the

Piscataway, New Jersey, school district. She brought suit against the Board of Edu-

cation because she was furloughed rather than a black teacher who was hired at the

same time with the same qualifications. A federal appeals court ruled that the school

board used racial bias in an employment decision because the black teacher was

"retained for diversity purposes" (Haworth). This court decision recognizes that the

**10**   civil rights of nonminorities are sacrificed when employers try to meet the demands

of affirmative action policies.

*Transitional
topic sentence*

In addition to being unfair to nonminorities, affirmative action policies have a

negative impact on employer's rights. Employers must be free from government reg-

ulations which mandate who can be hired, but this doesn't happen under the affir-

mative action guidelines. The workplace suffers when employers are forced to hire

minorities to fill a government imposed quota ("Not So Fast"). It's good business

sense to hire the best person for the job, not the candidate who is second or third

best. Government interference in the free market creates problems, as described in

a recent American Spectator article. Author James Bovard states that the U.S. Labor

**20**   Department's Office of Federal Contract Compliance Programs has become a "mon-

ster" that has "victimized" major corporations such as Siecor, Commonwealth Alu-

minum, and Carolina Steel in an attempt to enforce affirmative action hiring guide-

lines (38). This type of government regulation of business is unnecessary and

*Example and
explanation to
support the point
that affirmative
action is unfair*

*To cite article with
no author given, use
shortened title. See
pages 73–74.*

*Expert opinion*

*Cite only page
number when
author's name is
used in text*

Benson 3

**1**   nonproductive. Minorities are speaking out against affirmative action policies.

Ward Connerly, co-chairman of the American Civil Rights Institute, believes

that businesses should not be regulated by the government's quest for diversity. He      *Expert opinion*

*Square brackets*      states, "As a entrepreneur, I wanted to hear [politicians] talk about my needs as a
*used to indicate*
*change in wording*      black person being no different than anybody else's needs" (qtd. in Bray). Affirmative
*of quotation.*
*See pages 62–63*      action programs cause the government to misuse its power which has a detrimental
*and 115.*
impact on American business. Tax money is wasted on federal investigators and

government bureaucrats who check the personnel records of American businesses

(Becker). Tax payers know that this money should be spent on programs that would

**10**   ease some of our national problems such as the improvement of education or the      *Readers can*
                                                                                          *relate to these*
reduction of crime.                                                                       *concerns*

Another difficulty with affirmative action is that it creates uneasiness among

members of society. Continued attempts to enforce quotas will result in a divided

society (Nelton). In the workplace tension results when coworkers believe that mi-

norities were hired to fill quotas. When employees face stressful life threatening situ-

ations, as seen in police work, racial quotas add to an already difficult situation.

Some police officers wonder if the new minority officer met the entrance require-
*No page number*
*needed in citation*      ments or was given the job because of a quota system (Becker). Minorities also ex-
*for one-page article*
perience the tension created by affirmative action. Successful black professionals

**20**   are resentful when their colleagues assume that they are of "lower quality than a

white in the same position" (Scanlan 39). Americans know that racial quotas create

problems, so it is time for the government to recognize that affirmative action poli-      *Restatement of*
                                                                                          *thesis used to keep*
cies create division among the races. When will our lawmakers realize that federal        *paper focused*

Benson 4

**1** guidelines cannot guarantee racial harmony?

Affirmative action not only causes racial division, but it actually hurts those it *Transitional topic sentence*
was designed to help. Because quotas specify how many minorities an employer

must hire, minority professionals who were hired on the basis of merit are included in

quotas. This means that well-qualified professionals are treated as tokens. Ernest van *Expert opinion*

den Haag, a retired professor of jurisprudence at Fordham University Law School,

states in his essay "Affirmative Action and Campus Racism" that black members of

the faculty who worked hard to achieve a professional position are perceived as inad-

equate, as someone who was hired merely to fill a quota (177). This impropriety dam-

**10** ages an individual's self respect, the sense of being a well-qualified professional. Gary *Expert opinion*

A. Franks, a member of the U.S. House of Representatives and an African American,

comments on the federal guidelines for set-asides in hiring: "I do not want someone

to put their thumb on the scale in order for [my children] to succeed" (qtd. in Nelton

24). Franks means that he would like his children, as well as all minority children, to

succeed because they have worked hard, not because they are filling a quota.

Supporters of affirmative action respond by claiming that working hard is not *Counter-argument #1*

enough. Discriminatory practices have prevented well-qualified minorities from get-

ting jobs. According to an article in <u>Black Enterprise</u>, in the past minority graduates

received fewer job interviews than whites, even though they were well qualified

**20** (Conrad 24). This type of discrimination may have been a part of the past, but *Refutation*

today's companies are concerned about their public images. In addition, they know

that a diversified, multiracial work force best reflects the population of the United

States. In fields ranging from law enforcement and health care to teaching and retail-

Benson 5

**1**    ing, minorities are needed (Schrag 14). The federal government needs to recognize,

however, that businesses must make their own hiring decisions and should not be

subject to the negative impact of affirmative action.

Those in favor of affirmative action claim that the policies are essential to the          *Counter-*
*argument #2*
advancement of minorities. Supporters believe that government regulations are

needed to promote minorities who were victimized by society so they will benefit

economically and socially. According to Amselle, author of "A Quota By Any Other

Name," historians and economists note that minorities were not given equal oppor-

tunities in the workplace and were forced to search for lower paying jobs and suffer

**10**   economically as a result of low incomes. They found that blacks suffered socially          *Refutation*

due to the false notion that they were unequal to whites (21–4). Most Americans

readily recognize that minorities faced impediments to their advancement, but affir-

mative action is not the answer. Supporters state that the unfair treatment that non-

minorities experience is justified because it is for the good of the public, despite the

burdens it imposes (Nagel 180). Reverse discrimination, however, doesn't correct the

injustices of the past. The government's attempt to correct the historical legacy of

prejudice by discriminating against other groups is wrong.                                  *Restatement of thesis*

Before becoming a college student, I worked in a tool and die plant where I

observed the ill effects of affirmative action. To meet a government quota, the man-

**20**   agement hired a minority worker to run a 7,000-pound press. After two months of        *Personal*
*experience to*
training and careful supervision, the employee was not successful in the job. The         *support thesis*

plant manager was reluctant to assign the man to a less-skilled, lower-paying posi-

tion because government regulations labeled this as "discrimination." The situation

Benson 6

**1**     frustrated the manager and made the worker feel inadequate. The result was that

the minority worker quit, and I know that his self-esteem was damaged by this expe-

rience, which was designed by the federal government to give him equal opportuni-

ties.

        This country has experienced a number of serious political and legal attacks

against affirmative action plans. In fact, affirmative action policies are being chal-

lenged successfully in the courts. In one case, the U.S. Court of Appeals ruled that

the University of Texas law school could no longer use minority quotas as part of the

admissions standards. According to this decision, an institution faces financial

**10**    penalties if the admissions or financial aid awards are racially based (Lederman

A41). These rulings mean that minorities cannot be given preferential treatment, sug-

gesting that our lawmakers now recognize that equality cannot be legislated. A 1996

Supreme Court decision attempted to work against the problem of reverse discrimi-

nation. The court anticipated a backlash against affirmative action programs and

ruled in favor of a white-owned company that suffered economically when a minority

company won a government contract due to a federal program (Barinaga and Kaiser

1908). These court decisions recognize that racial preferences cause tension and

that government regulations cannot create racial harmony. It's time to recognize that

affirmative action has a negative impact on society.

**20**            In addition to court decisions against affirmative action, voters are showing

that preferences must stop. California's Civil Rights Initiative, known as Proposition

209, works against race-based admissions and hiring. In 1996, a substantial majority

of California voters approved this ballot measure, signaling the end to preferential

*See use of "I"*
*pages 106–107.*

*Present status*
*of affirmative*
*action*

*Restatement of*
*thesis*

1
treatment (Bray 5B). Of course, this is a step in the right direction, but the anti-

affirmative action movement needs to continue throughout the entire country. Let

people prove themselves by their accomplishments, not by their race.

Benson 8

Works Cited

**1**  Amselle, Jay. "A Quota By Any Other Name." <u>National Review</u> 26 Feb. 1996: 20+.

Barinaga, Marcia and Jocelyn Kaiser. "Backlash Strikes at Affirmative Action Pro-

grams." <u>Science</u> 271: 5257 (1996) 1908–10.

Becker, Gary S. "End Affirmative Action As We Know It." <u>Business Week</u> 21 Aug.

1995: 16.

Bovard, James. "Here Comes the Goon Squad." <u>American Spectator</u> July 1996:

36+.

Bray, Thomas J. "A Crisis of Confidence in Academia." <u>Detroit News</u> 9 Mar. 1997:

6B.

**10**  Conrad, Cecilia. "College Grads and Affirmative Action." <u>Black Enterprise</u> 26 (1995):

24.

Haworth, Karla. "Federal Court Ruling in N. J. Deals Another Blow to Affirmation Ac-

tion in Education." <u>Chronicle of Higher Education</u> 6 Sept. 1996: A57.

Lederman, Douglas. "Educators and Lawmakers in Texas Seek New Ways to Help

Minority Students." <u>Chronicle of Higher Education</u> 22 Nov. 1996: A27+.

Nagel, Thomas. "A Defense of Affirmative Action." QQ 1981. Rpt. in <u>Current Issues

and Enduring Questions</u> Ed. Sylvan Barnet and Hugo Bedau. Boston: St.

Martin's, 1993. 179–83.

Nelton, Sharon. "Minority Set-Asides: Change Ahead." <u>Nation's Business</u> Oct. 1995:

**20**  24.

"Not So Fast." <u>New York Times</u> 29 Dec. 1996: E2. <u>New York Times Online</u>.  Online.        *Entry for online*
                                                                                                 *source*
Nexis. 11 Feb. 1997.

1

Scanlan, James P. "The Curious Case of Affirmative Action for Women." <u>Society</u> 29

(1992): 36–41.

Schrag, Peter. "Backing off Bakke: The New Assault on Affirmative Action." <u>Nation</u>,

22 Apr. 1996: 11+.

Van den Haag, Ernest. "Affirmative Action and Campus Racism." Academic Ques-

tions 1989. Rpt. in <u>Current Issues and Enduring Questions</u> Ed. Sylvan Barnet

and Hugo Bedau. Boston: St. Martin's, 1993. 175–78.

# CHAPTER **12**

# APA Documentation Style

## USING APA DOCUMENTATION

The American Psychological Association (APA) documentation style is designed to provide easy, concise reference to sources cited in a paper. This style is used by various fields within the natural and social sciences as well as in other academic disciplines. This chapter explains the APA style and provides examples of parenthetical citations and reference list entries. A sample research essay titled "Pain Management for Cancer Patients" illustrates these guidelines. For further reference on APA documentation, refer to the following manual:

> American Psychological Association. <u>Publication Manual of the American Psychological Association</u>. 4th ed. Washington, D.C.: APA, 1994.

### Using the Appropriate Verb Tense

For papers written with APA documentation, use past tense or present perfect tense when you refer to a source cited in your paper. You should recognize that this style differs from the present tense verbs required of papers written with MLA documentation. Review the following examples:

| | | |
|---|---|---|
| APA | White *noted* that the results were not valid. | Past Tense |
| APA | White *has noted* that the results were not valid. | Present Perfect |
| MLA | White *notes* that the results *are* not valid. | Present Tense |

There is an exception to this guideline: Use present tense to present the results of a study (the information *reveals*) or to present established knowledge (the experiment *provides*) when using the APA style. This is illustrated in the following sentence:

Murphy, Morris, and Lang (1997) *reported* that a survey of            Past Tense
1,200 physicians who treated cancer patients revealed that
85 percent *believe* that their patients did not receive                      Present Tense
adequate medication for pain.

## FORMAT FOR PARENTHETICAL CITATIONS

When using the American Psychological Association (APA) style, the citations in your paper should focus on the author and the date of the source. For quotations present the page number, preceded by "p." (for one page). Use "pp." for more than one page. Remember that you must use a citation to identify quotations, paraphrases, and summaries which were taken from sources.

If you use a table, graph, chart, or figure from a source, present the complete bibliographic information after the item. See the sample paper in this chapter for examples of how to cite these items.

Review the following examples of in-text citations for the APA style:

### *AUTHOR NAMED IN SENTENCE*

Jadad and Brown (1995) discovered that pain management affects four aspects of a patient's life.

According to Wilson (1996), the World Health Organization's guidelines were simple and well validated.

The U. S. Department of Health and Human Services (1997, p. 8) reported that many patients "lost hope when pain emerges, believing that pain heralds the inexorable progress of a feared, destructive, and fatal disease."   Page number needed for quotation.
End quotation with a period followed
by the quotation marks.

### *AUTHOR NAMED IN CITATION*

Recent research indicated that the psychological impact of pain is tremendous for the debilitated patient (Murphy, Morris, & Lang, 1997).

Approximately 30 percent of cancer patients do not suffer from pain (Forrest, 1994).

Pain management requires medical professionals to "seek an integrated approach which combines the skills of health care givers from across the disciplines" (Wahl & Jones, 1997, p. 88).   Page number needed for quotation.
Citation follows the quotation marks and ends with a period.

### *MORE THAN ONE SOURCE IN A CITATION*

List the sources in alphabetical order by author's last name. This is the same order in which they will appear in the list of references. Use semicolons to separate each source as shown:

A new awareness has developed as medical schools are educating oncologists about the treatment of pain (Forrest, 1994; Saidman, 1995).

## FORMAT FOR REFERENCE LIST

The list of sources that you have used in your paper is called the *References* list. This alphabetical listing should include only the sources cited in the paper. (The list is called the *Bibliography* if you are listing all of the sources you read for background information in addition to those cited in the paper.) Here are some guidelines for preparing the list of references:

1. Present the title "References" two spaces below the page number.
2. Double-space the list within entries as well as between entries. Notice that the first line is indented and the second line is flush with the left margin.
3. List the sources alphabetically by author's last name. Alphabetize corporate authors by the first major word. Use the title if the author is unknown. Omit "a," "an," and "the" when alphabetizing titles. Present the author's last name, followed by initials.
4. List names for all authors, noting that "et al." is not used in the list of references.
5. Capitalize proper nouns and the first words in titles and subtitles of books and articles. Use lowercase for the other words. Capitalize the names of periodicals.

### Book by a Single Author

The entry consists of three parts: Author, title, and publication information. Begin by listing the author's last name and the initials for the first name. Follow this with the date of publication in parentheses. The title of the work, which is underlined, appears next. Note that only the first word in the title or in any subtitle is capitalized. (Proper nouns should be capitalized also.) The place of publication and the publisher's name are presented last.

> Achebe, C. (1994). <u>Things fall apart</u>. New York: Doubleday.
>
> Nicholas, L. H. (1995). <u>The rape of Europa: The fate of Europe's treasures in the Third Reich and the Second World War</u>. New York: Random House.
>
> Rosenberg, T. (1995). <u>The haunted land: Facing Europe's ghosts after Communism</u>. New York: Random House.

### Work in a Book or Anthology

When using a selection from a book or an anthology, begin the entry with the author's name, the publication date, and the title of the selection. Note that the title of the selection is not in quotation marks. Present the author or editor's name, followed by the title of the book and page numbers. End with the publication information.

> Bloom, A. (1992). On a Greek holiday. In R. Haleton (Ed.), <u>Encountering cultures: Readings and writings in a changing world</u> (pp. 384–394). Boston: Blair Press.

## Periodicals

*Periodicals*, which are publications printed on a regular basis, include journals, magazines, and scholarly newsletters. Use the following format when preparing a reference list entry for periodicals.

Present the author's last name and use initials for the first name. When listing the title of the article, use uppercase letters for the first word and for proper nouns. For the periodical, use both uppercase and lowercase letters.

For journals, magazines, and newsletters, present the volume number. Present the issue number only if each issue begins on page one. Underline the title of the periodical and the volume number. If a volume number is not given, provide the month or season. Provide the page numbers, but only use the designations "p." and "pp." for newspapers.

Franklin, J. E. (1995). Addiction medicine. <u>Journal of the American Medical Association,</u>
<u>273</u>, 1656–1657.
Volume Number

Kneese, C. C. (1996). Review of research on student learning in year-round education. <u>Journal</u>
<u>of Research and Development in Education, 29</u>, 60-72.
                              Volume Number

Lagnado, L. (1996, August 20). But who will pay for the high cost of relief? <u>Wall Street Journal</u>,
p. 81.
Use "p." for newspapers

Thomas, E. (1997, June 2). The plan and the man. <u>Newsweek</u>, 36–39.

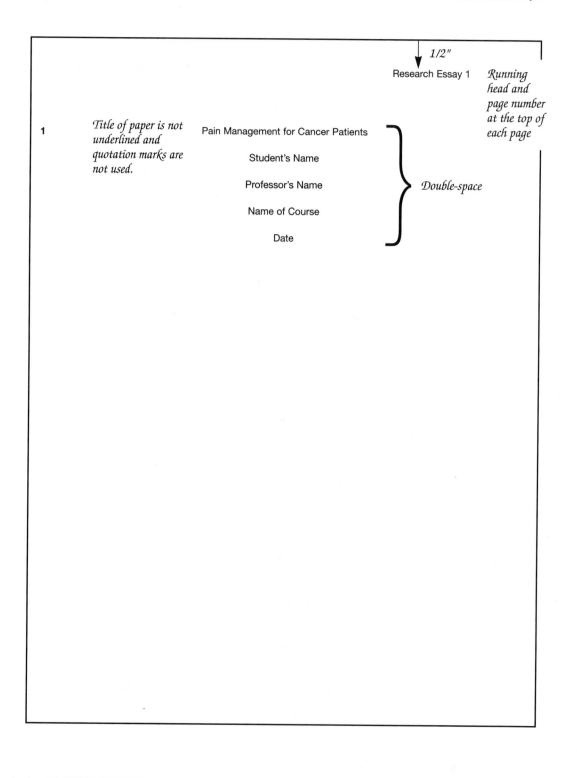

1/2"

Research Essay 1

*Running head and page number at the top of each page*

1    *Title of paper is not underlined and quotation marks are not used.*

Pain Management for Cancer Patients

Student's Name

Professor's Name

Name of Course

Date

*Double-space*

*Abstract is presented on page 2.*
*The length should be from*
*100–120 words.*

Research Essay 2

Abstract

*Do not*
**1**      *indent*  ◄——— This study investigated the control and management of cancer pain by health

care professionals. Advancements have been made within the past ten years, yet

undermedication remains a problem for a large number of cancer patients. The rea-

sons for inadequate pain management relate to the misperceptions of health care

professionals regarding the side effects of analgesics. Other difficulties relate to the

patient's reluctance to report discomfort and to take medications. The World Health

Organization attempted to provide guidelines for treating pain, yet this information

has not been effective. Future studies call for research into new areas of pain

**10**      therapy.

Research Essay 3

Pain Management for Cancer Patients  ◄─────────── *Center title.*
*Do not underline*
*or use quotation*
*marks*

**1**          Each year over one million Americans are diagnosed with cancer. Even though

the treatment of cancer pain has advanced within the past ten years, the control and

management of pain remains a problem. The progress that has been made can be         ⎫ *Passive*

attributed to several factors. Most significantly, patients and families have demanded   ⎭ *voice*

that pain be managed, resulting in a greater understanding by health care profes-

sionals of the need to control symptoms to improve the patient's quality of life. In

addition, some advancements in the understanding of the use of analgesic drugs

have occurred.

────────── *Underline headings*

Understanding Cancer Pain  ◄────

**10**          Approximately 30 percent of cancer patients do not suffer from pain (Forrest,

*Author and date*   1994). For those patients who do experience pain, however, the discomfort generally
*are separated*
*by comma in*      is the result of the tumor infiltrating the bones and other tissues. The pain is aggra-
*APA style.*
vated by primary cancer therapies such as surgery, chemotherapy, and radiotherapy

or by diagnostic procedures such as the CT scan, MRI, or myelogram.

Medical professionals acknowledged that not all cancer pain and the associ-

ated symptoms can be eliminated entirely, but they know that most patients can ex-

perience some pain relief. The U.S. Department of Health and Human Services

*Present year if* ──▶ (1997) noted that cancer pain is frequently undertreated in adults. Physicians are be-
*author appears*
*in text*         ginning to recognize that undermedication is a problem. Murphy, Morris, and Lang

**20**          (1997) reported that a survey of 1,200 physicians who treated cancer patients re-

**1**

vealed that 85 percent believed that their patients did not receive adequate medica-

tion for pain.

The reasons for inadequate pain management relate to problems with health

care professionals and the health care system as well as to problems involving patients

*Reference to table*

(Table 1). The health care professional may not adequately assess the pain or may be-

come too concerned about the side effects of analgesics and the possible addiction to

controlled substances. In a similar manner, pain may not be controlled because the pa-

tient fails to report the discomfort and may be reluctant to take pain medications.

*Identify table*

Table 1   Barriers to Cancer Pain Management

**10**

Problems related to health care professionals
   Inadequate knowledge of pain management
   Poor assessment of pain
   Concern about regulation of controlled substances
   Fear of patient addiction
   Concern about side effects of analgesics
Concern about patients becoming tolerant to analgesics
Problems related to patients
   Reluctance to report pain
     Concern about distracting physicians from treating disease

**20**

     Fear that pain means disease is worse
     Concern about not being a "good" patient
   Reluctance to take pain medications
     Fear of addiction or of being thought of as an addict
     Worries about unmanageable side effects
     Concern about becoming tolerant to pain medications
Problems related to health care system
   Low priority given to cancer pain treatment
   Inadequate reimbursement
     Most appropriate treatment may be too costly

**30**

   Restrictive regulation of controlled substances
   Problems of availability of treatment or access to it

*Identify source of table*

*Note:* From <u>Clinical Practice Guideline: Management of Cancer Pain</u>,
by the U.S. Department of Health and Human Services, 1997, p. 17.

*Double-space*

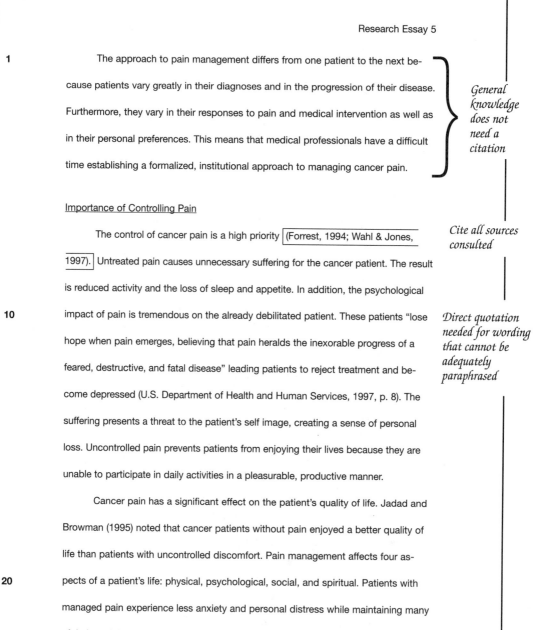

Research Essay 5

**1**      The approach to pain management differs from one patient to the next be-

cause patients vary greatly in their diagnoses and in the progression of their disease.

Furthermore, they vary in their responses to pain and medical intervention as well as

in their personal preferences. This means that medical professionals have a difficult

time establishing a formalized, institutional approach to managing cancer pain.

*General knowledge does not need a citation*

Importance of Controlling Pain

     The control of cancer pain is a high priority (Forrest, 1994; Wahl & Jones,

1997). Untreated pain causes unnecessary suffering for the cancer patient. The result

is reduced activity and the loss of sleep and appetite. In addition, the psychological

*Cite all sources consulted*

**10**      impact of pain is tremendous on the already debilitated patient. These patients "lose

hope when pain emerges, believing that pain heralds the inexorable progress of a

feared, destructive, and fatal disease" leading patients to reject treatment and be-

come depressed (U.S. Department of Health and Human Services, 1997, p. 8). The

suffering presents a threat to the patient's self image, creating a sense of personal

loss. Uncontrolled pain prevents patients from enjoying their lives because they are

unable to participate in daily activities in a pleasurable, productive manner.

*Direct quotation needed for wording that cannot be adequately paraphrased*

     Cancer pain has a significant effect on the patient's quality of life. Jadad and

Browman (1995) noted that cancer patients without pain enjoyed a better quality of

life than patients with uncontrolled discomfort. Pain management affects four as-

**20**      pects of a patient's life: physical, psychological, social, and spiritual. Patients with

managed pain experience less anxiety and personal distress while maintaining many

of their social and physical activities.

Research Essay 6

World Health Issue

**1**      The World Health Organization (WHO) has recognized that pain management

is a significant issue in the public health of developing and developed countries. The

organization provided a set of guidelines on cancer pain relief known as the "three-

step analgesic ladder" (Figure 1). According to Jadad and Browman (1995), these

guidelines are based on the following premise:

*5 spaces* ⟶ [M]ost patients throughout the world should have adequate pain relief if
health care providers learn how to use a few effective and relatively inexpen-
sive drugs well and administer them by mouth, on a regular basis, and according to the individual needs of each patient. (p. 1870)

*Indent extended quotation and omit quotation marks*

*Page number after period.*

**10**      The WHO information on pain management was widely disseminated, having

*No period after parenthesis*

been distributed in twenty-two languages throughout the world. Even though the

guidelines were simple and well validated, research indicated that most cancer pa-

tients were not receiving adequate pain relief (Wilson, 1996; Wahl & Jones, 1997).

The conclusion is that the WHO analgesic ladder is not as effective as believed and

that achieving pain relief is more complex than medical professionals thought.

Figure 1

**World Health Organization Analgesic Ladder**

3   **Freedom from Cancer Pain**
      Strong Opioid for Moderate to Severe Pain
**20**        +Nonopioid
       +Adjuvant

2   **Pain Persisting or Increasing**
      Weak Opioid for Mild to Moderate Pain
      +Nonopioid
      +Adjuvant

1   **Pain Persisting or Increasing**
      Nonopioid
      +Adjuvant

*Note:* From "The WHO Analgesic Ladder for Cancer Pain Management," by
**30** A. R. Jadad and G. P. Browman, 1995, Journal of the American Medical Association,
274, p. 1871.

*Double-space*

*Identify source*

Research Essay 7

<u>Future Studies</u>

1

        Although medical professionals recognized the need for continued research into the management of cancer pain, no controlled studies have been conducted to determine the effectiveness of the analgesic ladder (Jadad and Browman, 1995). Future studies would reveal if the WHO guidelines are improving the management of cancer pain.

        Recent research and publications (Wilson, 1996) encouraged clinicians to become more active in integrating advances in pain therapy. The goal is to provide an across the disciplines approach by using the expertise of professionals ranging from anesthesiologists, neurosurgeons, and rheumatologists to psychiatrists and psychol-

10

ogists. A new awareness has developed as medical schools are educating oncologists about the treatment of pain (Forrest, 1994; Saidman, 1995). Other advances include studies of the psychological methods for relieving pain such as imagery, hypnosis, and relaxation.

*1/2"*

*Indent first line of
each entry five
1     spaces* ───▶ References

Forrest, J. B. (1994). Conquering pain. Hamilton, Canada: Empowering Press.

Jadad, A. R. & Browman, G. P. (1995). The WHO analgesic ladder for cancer

pain management. Journal of the American Medical Association, 274, 1870–73.       *Present entries
in alphabetical
order*

Murphy, G. P., Morris, L. B., & Lange, D. (1997). Informed decisions: The

complete book of cancer diagnosis, treatment, and recovery. New York: Viking

Press.

Saidman, L. J. (1995). Anesthesiology. Journal of the American Medical Asso-       *Double-space*

ciation, 273, 1661–62.

U.S. Department of Health and Human Services. (1997). Clinical practice

10     guideline: Management of cancer pain. Washington, D.C.: Public Health Service.

Wahl, T. T. & Jones, M. (1997, September 12). Fighting cancer pain. Science

News, 44. (DIALOG file 668: MAGAZINE ASAP, Item 8198).

Wilson, R. R. (1996). [Review of the book Pain management: Theory and

practice]. New England Journal of Medicine, 335, 904.                              ◀──────▶
                                                                                   *One inch*

◀──────▶
*One inch*

# APPENDIX A

# Reference Sources

## General Indexes

*Academic Index*
*Infotrac*
*Wilsondisc (select subject areas)*
*Reader's Guide to Periodicals Index*
Opening text

*New York Times Index*
*Washington Post Index*
*Wall Street Journal Index*
*CBS News Index*

## Specialized Sources

### GENERAL SOURCES FOR ART

*Guide to the Literature of Art History*
*Encyclopedia of World Art*
*Art Research Methods and Resources:*
  *A Guide to Finding Art Information*
*Annotated Bibliography of Fine Art*

•

### ELECTRONIC SOURCES FOR ART

*Arts & Humanities Search*
*Artbibliographies Modern*
*Art Literature International (RILA)*
*Wilsondisc: Art Index*

### GENERAL SOURCES FOR BIOLOGY

*Biology Data Book*
*Encyclopedia of the Biological Sciences*
*Encyclopedia of Bioethics*
*Information Sources in the Life Sciences*
*Magill's Survey of Science: Life Science Series*
*Biological Abstracts*
*General Science Index*

### ELECTRONIC SOURCES FOR BIOLOGY

*Acricola*
*Aquaculture*

*Biosis Previews*
*Scisearch*
*Wilsondisc: Biological & Agricultural Index*

**GENERAL SOURCES FOR BUSINESS**

*Business Periodicals Index*
*Dictionary of Business and Management*
*Business Information Sources*
*Historical Bibliography of Administration, Business, and Management*
*Bibliographic Guide to Business and Economics*

**ELECTRONIC SOURCES FOR BUSINESS**

*Wilsondisc: Business Periodicals Index*
*Economic Literature Index*
*Trade and Industry Index*
*Standard & Poor's Index*
*Business Index*

**GENERAL SOURCES FOR EDUCATION**

*Encyclopedia of Educational Research*
*International Encyclopedia of Education*

*Library Research Guide to Education*
*Education Journals and Serials*
*Education: A Guide to Reference and Information Sources*
*Wilsondisc: Education Index*

**ELECTRONIC SOURCES FOR EDUCATION**

*ERIC*
*Education Index*
*Current Index to Journals in Education*

**GENERAL SOURCES FOR HISTORY**

*Dictionary of American History*
*Handbook for Research in American History*
*Library Research Guide to History*

**ELECTRONIC SOURCES FOR HISTORY**

*America: History and Life*
*Humanities Index*
*American Historical Association*

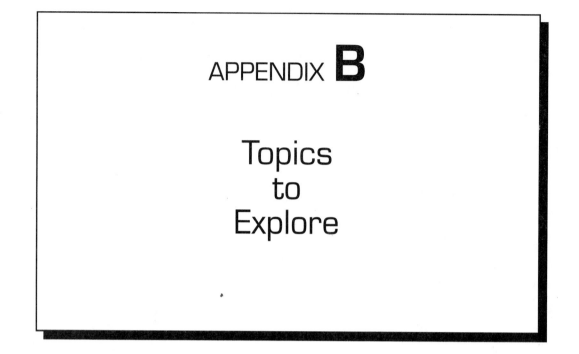

# APPENDIX B

# Topics to Explore

*Internet Indecency:* It's a struggle between free speech and the need to protect children from pornographic materials via the Internet. Is the Communications Decency Act an unconstitutional violation of free speech? Should Internet carriers make money by selling pornography to children? Is it the family's responsibility to keep children away from online smut?

*Organ Donation and Transplants:* Medical advancements have made organ donations possible, saving the lives of thousands. The issue of organ donation, however, is complicated because of a shortage of viable organs. Who should receive a heart or a kidney? Should celebrities and those who can pay be moved to the head of the lengthy waiting list? Are organ transplants only for the wealthy?

*Home Schooling:* Thousands of children do not attend school because their parents have chosen home schooling, a practice that has many advantages. Critics of home schooling, however, claim that the young people suffer academically as well as socially. Do the positive factors outweigh the negative points?

*Labor Unions:* In the early days, labor unions protected workers from unsafe working conditions and unfair managerial practices. Times have changed and critics of organized labor argue that unions are detrimental because they inflate wages and protect unmotivated workers. Union supporters, by contrast, argue that management takes advantage of workers. Do you support labor unions?

***Victim Impact Statements:*** Many states allow victims to address the court before the accused is sentenced, believing that victims need the opportunity to express their rage and sense of loss. Other states believe that victim impact statements turn the courtroom into an emotional circus. Should victim impact statements be allowed in the courtroom? Are they as effective as advocates of victims' rights would like them to be?

***College Sports:*** Universities become involved in a sports scandal because gifts are given to athletes, and many wonder if the rules are too restrictive. They argue that athletes are entitled to benefits because their performance brings money to their university. Defenders of the present system claim that allowing college athletes to receive gifts damages the amateur status of college sports. What is your position?

***Underage Drinking:*** Because of serious problems with alcohol abuse and binge drinking, many colleges and universities are reviewing their policies on underage drinking. Some institutions, such as the University of Delaware, have a new approach which includes notifying parents. In addition, freshmen and sophomores are suspended from on-campus housing for three violations, while juniors and seniors are suspended from the university for two violations. The new policies are controversial because critics believe that the institution should not regulate student behavior. Should campus regulations punish underage drinkers? Will the restrictions solve the problem of binge drinking?

***Police Brutality:*** Police brutality in American cities has become a nationwide problem, requiring police departments to adopt new approaches to law enforcement. Is it possible to reduce the number of racially related cases of police brutality?

***Poverty in the United States:*** Within the past ten to twenty years, thousands of full-time workers have become part of the "working poor." These people do not qualify for government assistance because their income is above the official poverty level. Is the government responsible for revising its policies? Should these families be responsible for solving their own problems?

***Casino Gambling:*** Casino gambling has become an attractive form of entertainment while earning thousands of dollars in tax revenue. Those opposed to this form of recreation claim that it brings crime into a city while causing serious consequences for gamblers and their families. What's your opinion? Should casino gambling remain legal?

***Restricting Teen Drivers:*** The Center for Disease Prevention and Control indicates a high fatality rate for drivers between ages sixteen to twenty. Many states have responded by enacting new laws to restrict teen driving. Critics claim that the regulations are discriminatory. Should teen drivers face greater restrictions?

*Teen Pregnancy:* New welfare reform laws require states to prohibit sex between an adult and a minor as well as between minors. This means that pregnant
teenagers and their boyfriends can be charged with sex-related crimes. What is your
view of this new approach to the problem of teen pregnancy?

*Physician Assisted Suicide:* The issue of physician assisted suicide has caused
serious controversy because advocates believe that terminally ill patients have the
right to say when they want to die. Those opposed, however, believe that physicians'
licenses should be revoked if they comply with a patient's death wish. Should citizens
vote to show their support or disapproval of physician assisted suicide?

*Medical Marijuana:* What is the medical utility of marijuana? Should doctors
be allowed to prescribe marijuana to cancer patients for treatment of pain and nausea?
Should marijuana be kept illegal to restrict its use?

*Undocumented Workers:* Some employers hire illegal immigrants, claiming that
no one else will perform the low wage jobs. Should these employers face fines and
jail terms? Should undocumented workers be allowed to remain in this country?

*Ethics and Journalists:* Are journalists ethical? The journalistic styles of several popular documentary programs have been examined, and their motives are being
questioned. Does the media suffer from a liberal bias? Are journalists guilty of ex-
aggeration and overreporting?

*Anti-Fur Activists:* Animal rights groups have declared war on mink ranches,
and the FBI has responded by classifying these groups as domestic terrorist organizations. Are the anti-fur activists justified? What is the government's responsibility?

*Business Ethics and Product Liability:* Who is responsible for faulty products?
Should an automobile manufacturer be held liable for a design flaw that injures or
causes death? Has litigation gone too far, making lawyers wealthy because of years
of legal battles in the name of consumer rights?

*Business Ethics and Environmental Concerns:* Recent studies by the Citizens
Fund reveal that almost 75 percent of American manufacturers make no attempt to
prevent pollution or to reduce the use of toxic chemicals. Should citizens speak out
against this type of corporate irresponsibility? Has this become a political issue because business controls legislation?

*Business Ethics and Corporate Responsibility:* Some American companies
have closed inner-city factories and moved their facilities to Mexico. Although this
move saves money for a company, it causes thousands to become unemployed. What
is a corporation's responsibility? Should they think about social responsibility instead
of the bottom line?

***Computers in the Classroom:*** School districts throughout the United States are embracing high-technology as evidenced by the $4 billion price tag for computer expenses. The question of the effectiveness of computers in the classroom remains unresolved. Do students need computers? Does Internet access improve education? Should thousands of dollars be spent on high-tech equipment?

***Teens and Shopping Malls:*** Some states have considered passing laws that would allow local authorities to require teenagers under age sixteen to be accompanied by an adult when they go to malls during given hours. Supporters of this proposed legislation state that teens disturb other shoppers and create an unpleasant environment that isn't good for business. The opposition claims that such regulation is unfair because it punished all teens for the unacceptable conduct of a few. Is this legislation reasonable? Should laws be passed to restrict teens? How does the general public view the situation?

***Financial Aid for Foreign Students:*** Should U.S. colleges and universities give preference to American students when distributing financial aid? Yale University, for example, guarantees the financial support of those accepted if they are American or Canadian. By contrast, Harvard University has a "need-blind" admissions policy that includes financial support for all needy students, including foreign students. Some educators and students criticize the policy of giving aid to Americans first, noting the hypocrisy of an institution that limits support while claiming a climate of intellectual excellence and a large foreign-student enrollment. Others claim that American taxpayers subsidize financial aid programs at both public and private institutions. Should aid be based on academic merit? Which approach is fiscally responsible and morally appropriate?

# Index